Girl, Get Your Lyfe!!!

Girl, Get Your *Lyfe!!!*

KJ Franklin
Co-Author: AM Collins

XULON PRESS

Xulon Press
2301 Lucien Way #415
Maitland, FL 32751
407.339.4217
www.xulonpress.com

© 2020 by KJ Franklin - Co-Author: AM Collins

All rights reserved solely by the author. The author guarantees all contents are original and do not infringe upon the legal rights of any other person or work. No part of this book may be reproduced in any form without the permission of the author. The views expressed in this book are not necessarily those of the publisher.

Unless otherwise indicated, Scripture quotations taken from the Common English Bible® (CEB) Copyright © 2010, 2011 by Common English Bible.™ Used by permission. All rights reserved worldwide.

Printed In The Unites States.

Paperback ISBN-13: 978-1-6312-9979-7
Ebook ISBN-13: 978-1-6312-9980-3

♡ ♡ ♡

Girl, Get Your Lyfe!!!

Have you ever felt that you were not worthy of life, for no true reason—well, maybe for a reason you were not really sure of? You have been totally successful in your career, you have jumped over mediocre obstacles and landed in a place that individuals only wish they could be, and yet, you felt worthless and wanted to give up everything—truly everything, including your life! Well, you are not alone. Many women experience this level of self-doubt, depression, or lack of motivated support at certain periods in their life. Most are afraid to admit to it; most secretly deal with it to avoid being the topic of happy hour or the subject of tea time. They gossip amongst family and friends because they have never experienced that deep level of pain or self-doubt for no known reason. Most are embarrassed to seek medical help due to the stigma that may follow.

Also, growing up in the church, you are encouraged to pray on it, have faith, and believe that feeling will go away. Sometimes, however, prayer is not enough. God created individuals with medical expertise to assist with mental, emotional, and physical ailments. Most mental disorders are not controlled by an on-and-off switch; they are triggered by multiple things or stressors.

People often unload heavily weighted problems on and individual without being courteous of that person's mental capacity. For example, pastors withhold a lot, and they are expected to be there for everyone in their congregation, but most people will look down on their pastor or turn their back and gossip if the pastor has a mental breakdown. At some point, everyone has to create boundaries, seek help, or get assistance once there's a realization that the load is too heavy. It's time for people to realize that a high percentage of the world suffers from some form of undiagnosed depression, anxiety, and much more due to the common demands of society, the American dream, and trying to keep up with social standards. The Bible has answers for every problem, but to understand these answers, accept them, and decide to follow the Bible takes a certain level of commitment most don't have. Realizing, owning, and defining your problem is the first step; seeking assistance is the next; then drawing closer and learning the Word of God can assist in recovery.

Social media plays a huge role in people's ability to accept and be open with their internal issues. They are too shy to say they lack something or cannot afford a certain lifestyle for fear of being placed in front. Social media makes people feel that they are supposed to be moving at a certain pace, living a certain lifestyle, or receiving certain blessings that may not be a part of God's plan for their lives. Not everybody is meant to be living like the Smiths or the Williams; you are a Johnson, live life in your own truth. People often begin to process things a certain way based on the tangible items they see on social media, and negative influences then begin to enter their mind, giving them the rush to find ways to achieve something that may not even be a reality for some. Living on social media can allow you to enter a mystical world of make believe, putting you in constant competition against others. It can fill you with extensive anxiety for no reason.

Social media has also made some people stagnant in their roles, relationships, purposes, and careers, due to the time it takes away from pursuing things that are vital to progress. The lifestyles social media presents are not only mentally mesmerizing, but viewing them can become addictive, a habit that we allow to control the choices we make. Just to fit in to what we feel is a trend, we often develop a trait of lying without notice. Sometimes the lie can even become too hard to keep up with, and anxiety and depression set in because you may now be caught up in a web of lies. The suicide rate has been noticeably increasing, and many are unsure why; but the constant pressure of life, the inability to keep up with the lifestyle we have been shown, and the lack of mental awareness may be the cause of the increase.

We sometime forget that we are supposed to follow and serve only one person; we need to answer to only one person. We are not supposed to be boastful and become wrapped up in tangible items, nor get caught up in our appearances, modeling for the "Gram," or allowing the comments of others to drive down our self-awareness and esteem. We forget God is the only one we need to impress by following His Word and way. The great thing is that God will forgive us. He keeps watch over us and protects us, even when we don't realize we are lost in the earthly beings of our world.

> "Pride lays people low, but those of humble spirit gain honor." Proverbs 29:23 (CEB)

Table of Contents

Introducing: Girl, Get Your Lyfe!!!	v
Ann	1
Mary	5
Renee	11
Stacy	16
Diana	21
Vanessa	29
Jamie	31
Amanda	38
Kai	41
Kelli	45
Samantha	47
Evelynn	50
Keisha	53
Simone	57
Girl, it's time for self-reflection!	62
Girl, What's Your Battle?	63
Closed Doors	67
Girl, Know Yourself	68
Girl, Don't Drown!	71
Girl, Are You Insecure?	73
Wife and Motherhood	74

Teach Me How to Love	79
Finding the Blessing in the Breakup	82
A Guide to Overcome a Separation	86
Learning Myself Worksheet	92
References/Sources Used	94

Ann

Living vicariously through my friend, I wanted the confidence instead of the hesitation that came along with relationships. The stories my friend told me of the many guys she encountered were very interesting, and I slightly envied her because I lacked that excitement in my life. I was fascinated with the attention she received but never questioned her reasons for not committing. At the time, I was a teenager with raging hormones and just wanted a relationship. I loved to read romance novels and wanted to experience all that came along with romance, but I was still afraid to step out, until one day, my friend introduced me to my current husband.

Due to his mild tendencies, my friend thought he would be a good start for me. Green to life, I rapidly fell head over heels, ignoring the fact that my friend introduced him to me to just to dip my foot in the dating pool. He and I were so in love. We casted out all relationships, and we made a few enemies because of our love for each other. He was all I needed and wanted. I was attentive to his every need, even if it included rebelling to what I once thought was wrong, disrespecting my mother and her house, and disregarding the needs and feelings of my best friends. He was my first love, my first sexual experience, and my soulmate.

Two years into the relationship, he proposed to me with a ring from the bubble gum machine. I didn't care; I was in love and nineteen years old. We both were trying to start a life and attend college, and I knew things would get better. I was so happy but blind at the same time. My friend was very direct, to the point that I avoided telling her things because I didn't understand her negativity toward my relationship. She was very hardcore because of her childhood, which brought out disdain toward men.

To this day, I am still unsure how I fell for him so hard. Could it have been the passing of my father, which left me clueless about how a man is supposed to treat or love a woman, or the fact that I was missing love from a male figure? Was it the abusiveness and rebellious behavior from my older brother? Perhaps this made me cling harder to my husband because he was the total opposite of my brother. I knew I didn't want a man like my brother or his friends, but I was embarrassingly turned on by some of their behavior.

I thought I had the perfect husband, as if that can be a true possibility. I heard many stories that women told about their relationships: crying because their boyfriend cheated on them and got another girl pregnant; sneaking to the free clinic because they contracted gonorrhea or chlamydia; wearing globs of concealer to cover up the bruises and black eyes their jealous boyfriend had given them; working hard to buy their boyfriend the latest clothes; having their boyfriend drop them off at work while he stunts in their new car and picks up chicks; getting verbally abused when their boyfriend could not get his drug fix; being raped by their boyfriend when he was sky high. I could never deal with a man like that. I could never be used and abused as such. I did not have time for the drama and heartbreak. I loved my safe selection of a man, a husband, my future, my child's father. He and I had the same thoughts and disregard of that type of behavior and the situations at hand. Never would I have to worry like those other women. Never would I feel the hurt and agony; never would I be the one lying on my best friend's floor, crying my eyes out over a poor selection of a man. I knew what I was doing, and I was very confident in my safe choice. I imagined a life of happiness.

Time went by, and he fell into a slump of depression and dropped out of school. So, I overcompensated to make him happy. He was my soulmate, the love of my life, my partner. I wanted him to be happy, and he was because he was in control; I was still blind to that fact. I eventually finished college and started my career, but my husband was still lost in what he wanted to do. That was okay; he needed my support, and I was there.

Finally, it was time to plan the wedding. I took care of everything—the cost, the planning, the rings—and one week before the wedding, he hesitated to tell me that he wasn't ready. Crushed, I begged for answers, talked it out with him, and assured him that we would be alright. He felt that he didn't have a support system and had not yet experienced life, but I reassured him that I was his support system and we could experience life together. Because I had such a great support system, my family and friends made my wedding magical. My mom even allowed us to stay in her vacant house after the wedding so we could start our life fresh and recoup from the cost. We were so very blessed and happy.

A few months after our wedding, that "soulmate" feeling faded, only because we had been oblivious to the work we need to do to become one. Although I had been raised in the church, I started following my husband's way of life, which did not incorporate the Word of God. Wanting my relationship to work, I turned a blind eye to many feelings I felt. My husband had several faults, but I ignored them, hoping they would get better. Instead, these faults changed the person I once was, and I became a stranger to myself. Later, I became pregnant, which brought so much joy to my husband and me. I thought to myself, *Babies are such blessings.* My husband was happy again. He found a job he loved and was promoted, then we purchased a home, and he even got himself a new car. Everything was going well.

As time passed, I began to notice a lack in communication between my husband and me; he was working more, but that was important for him to gain self-worth. My mom and my friend would frequently visit me, but they always made comments that repulsed me and made me question my marriage. They questioned my appearance, as if I was the only one out of us three who had gained weight. They made comments about my house always being dirty. I soon came to the point where I was okay with the way everything was and didn't want their company anymore. I found myself being by myself more, and it seemed that my husband had his own set of friends, something he had never wanted before. I had once been his only friend, his best friend, and he had told me we didn't need family and friends because we were enough for each other. I secretly resented him from pulling me away from my family and friends. Although he had said that we didn't have the money to go on dates, travel, or do anything, he began to spend our money on and with his friends. When he was home, he just ate, played video games, and screwed me, literally. I wasn't getting anything out of it. However, I kept my mouth closed, smiled, and remained the humble housewife, no matter how much my mother and best friend told me I was foolish.

We have been married twelve years, and I have yet to feel as if his love for me outweighs the love he has for *his* personal time. In all of our years of marriage, I never once remember him telling me to take a personal day or treat myself to something nice, or even springing for a nice gift for me. It was like he didn't care about me as a person.

You know, now that I am actually sitting down and thinking about it, my life is a damn cliché for a middle-aged housewife. How am I any different from any of those other women you hear about who devote their lives to their families and, in the end, are lonely and unhappy? I am unhappy now, and technically, this is just the beginning of our marriage.

Mary

Mary Thibodeaux stood in her room, glancing at her body in the mirror. She twisted this way and that way, looking at her butt and stomach, making sure she was presentable and all elements were in their correct places. Tonight was the night. Two years ago, she'd met her boyfriend, Jermaine, and promised him that if they lasted two years without cheating or breaking up, she would present him with her virginity. In her mind, Mary hoped that her precious gift would keep him with her, binding them together for life. Her parents were first loves who had married two years after graduating high school. Her father worked until her mother finished college, then he continued school and finished. They were not a perfect couple, but they were a great example of what working together for a family looked like.

Mary's parents did not like Jermaine. They tried to hide it, but she could tell. Her father, Paul, asked Jermaine questions, and rarely could Jermaine answer them, at least straightforward and honestly. What did her father expect? Jermaine was only seventeen, and her father wanted Jermaine to have all the answers in the universe. It was not possible.

"Mary?" her mother knocked on the door. "Mary?" She knocked again with more urgency. Mary's door was locked, and that never happened. "What's going on?"

"I... I'm coming, Mom." Mary gave herself one last look then walked to the door. She opened the door slowly.

"Girl, what are you doing in here?" her mother, Maize, griped. Mary stepped all the way back so her mother could enter her room. She braced herself for her mother's next words.

"Well now, Mary," Maize said, looking her daughter over, "what is this occasion you're dressed up for?"

"Oh, Mom," she said blushing, "Jermaine wants to take me out tonight."

"Oh, yeah?" Her mother looked into her eyes, squinting now. "What's the occasion, Mary?" her mother asked again, and Mary looked away before answering.

"Tonight is our two-year anniversary," she answered honestly.

"Two years, huh?"

"Yes," she turned to her mother, looking her in the eyes, emboldened by her decision to have sex. Maize nodded, looking around her daughter's room. At seventeen, Mary was an A student and on track to graduate with honors in four months. She had already been accepted into college at AMU. *Oh, but that boy Jermaine!* Maize shook her head thinking of him. Jermaine kept Mary's mind off her studies and into God knows what. Maize turned back to Mary. Her daughter stood boldly, and Maize felt chills on her arms; her face immediately felt warm. "Mary, whatever you are planning tonight, please, please rethink it."

Mary leaned her head slightly to the right side. "Why, Mom?" The question was not an innocent one, but one of knowledge and defiance.

Maize rushed to her daughter, holding her by her shoulders. "Mary, it would be a mistake. Please, daughter, I beg you, don't go through with your plans."

Mary gave her mom a sad, patronizing smile, "I plan to have dinner with my boyfriend, Mom. That is all."

Maize felt her hair rise as her daughter lied to her face, thinking she was outsmarting her mother with half-truths and sweet expressions. She jerked her hands away from her daughter. "Mary," she pointed to her daughter's chest, "I know you are planning to have sex tonight, and I know this is your first time." She took a deep breath as tears pierced her eyes. "I know you don't think I like Jermaine, but really, child, I just love you more. You are way beyond that boy!" Maize's emotions were building up, and she wanted to curb the disappointment her daughter would surely feel when the night did not go as planned.

"Mom, how could you say that? Jermaine has been trying! He graduates this year too, and he has plans, big plans!"

Maize shook her head at her daughter's ignorance. "Baby, do those plans include you?"

"Of course," Mary said quickly but quietly realized that she had not asked about or actually seen those plans, so she had no idea if Jermaine's plans included her…but her plans included him. Since Jermaine did not get into AMU, Mary would attend a college in town, and hopefully after a year of college, they could both transfer to a larger university. She nodded in agreement with her plans and smiled.

How could Maize get Mary to understand? *Jesus, please help me change her mind,* she silently called out.

"Paul!" Maize called out loud to her husband. "Paul!" she called again with urgency.

"Yeah, baby?" he called back.

"Talk to your daughter because she is not listening to me." There was a silence, and Mary wanted to crawl under her bed and wait for the time to pass. She never wanted to disappoint her parents, especially her father, who had taken the time to teach her so many things.

"Dad, everything is fine." Mary hoped to stop him from coming into her room. Neither Mary nor her mom heard footsteps, and Mary breathed a sigh of relief.

Mary woke up in pain, feeling shame. The light from the window filtered through her eyelids. She immediately felt pain below, and the memories from last night flooded back.

Jermaine picked her up as planned, but instead of heading to a restaurant, he drove her to a seedy part of town known for drugs and other crimes.

Jermaine parked at the hotel The Rosebud, in front of room 214, then turned off the car. Mary looked toward him.

"Why are we here? What happened to going to eat first?"

"Aww, baby, I was just so anxious to be with you. We can have dinner after, but I really want to be with you. I have thought of nothing else since you told me it was time." His eyes were so sincere and loving, all she could do was smile. She had been looking forward to this as well, but she wondered why he had chosen this place. It was not where she had imagined losing her virginity.

"Why here, though? I thought we were going to the hotel where your sister Mimi worked."

"Uh, she got fired, so I couldn't get that deal no more." He paused and took a breath. "Baby, I know what you are thinking, but this is what I could afford. You deserve so much more, but I wanted to make this night special. Please don't be disappointed." Mary searched his eyes with her own and found him honest. She gave another smile.

"Okay, Jermaine, but I was looking forward to sitting down across from you and sharing a meal. That was a part of my dream day with you."

Jermaine nodded, looking away. Mary did not see his clenching his fist. She took his looking away as silent disappointment and not growing impatience. Taking off her seatbelt, she waited for Jermaine to exit the car and come around to open the door for her. He had learned to do this over the past two years, and she smiled. Her mother had warned her that there were things she would need to train her husband to do, and Jermaine had obviously learned.

They exited the car, then Mary stood behind Jermaine while he unlocked the hotel room door; she felt uneasy—not the unease of anticipation, but the thought or feeling that something was wrong. She could not shake it, and it began as soon as she got into his car.

As they walked in the room, Mary immediately smelled old unwashed linens, sitting water, and dust. This was not what she had imagined. Her mind flickered back to the pictures online of the pricey hotel downtown where Jermaine's sister Mimi worked. They'd scoped out which room he would purchase for their first night, and she remembered Jermaine telling her last week that the room was already paid for and they were good to go. What happened, and why did he wait to tell her now? Looking around, Mary felt a volcano of disappointment welling up in her stomach, and her feeling of unease worsened. She knew her worth, and tonight, Jermaine reneged on her dream.

"I know this is not what we discussed, but we can make it beautiful," Jermaine knew he was losing Mary. He could feel her stiffening in his arms.

"I'm just trying to understand. What happened to the Marriott? You said the room was paid for."

"I know...I didn't want you to back out." He lowered his head. He'd practiced this in the mirror at home in case she asked about the room. She shook her head and walked over to him, touching his face. She'd already asked him, but she had to try to believe him. Was it worth it?

She smiled up at him. "Okay." She was giving up her dream, but she hoped they would be good.

Her dream of romance ended as soon she acquiesced. His tenderness faded and became rough. He pushed her toward the bed, and she stumbled backwards. His eyes changed, and what she had mistaken earlier for focus she realized too late was hate. He hated her! But why? She did not have to wait long for the answer.

"You made me wait too long, Mary. I was going to other girls for satisfaction." His smile now was sinister, and there were no good intentions in his eyes.

"Then why am I here?" She asked hoarsely, the shock of his revelation ringing in her ears. She pushed at him to get off of her, but he only laughed.

"You think you can fight me?"

Mary's breaths came out in short, panicked bursts. "Get off me, Jermaine. We are over. Let me up!" She looked at him in the eyes so that he could see how serious she was.

"Not until I get my fill."

There was no undressing or kisses behind her ear or on her neck. He groped and tugged and penetrated her forcefully. WHY?

When he was finished, he lay on top and offered a final blow: "Who will want you now?!" He laughed as he pulled out of her.

Mary lay frozen as he dressed in the bathroom. She could hear him moving around, but she was too dazed and confused. She almost laughed.

"Why you still lying down?" He chuckled. "Well I guess, I put it on you!" He did not care that he had just raped her, and she could tell that he did not see this as wrong. She needed to get home, take a shower, and pray that she would never see him again.

I need to tell someone, Mary thought. I need to go to the doctor...the pain is excruciating. I don't think he used protection. Should he be jailed for rape? But the embarrassment from it all settled in. I boasted about how great Jermaine was to my friends, my mother, and my father, knowing no one trusted or liked him for me. I wanted to prove them wrong so badly... it turns out they all were right. I would never have thought that after two years, he could be this sick and evil. I will take this secret to the grave. I will never talk to him again—as a matter of fact, no man ever again. I can't believe I lost my virginity in this manner.

God, please forgive me. I know I rebelled against You and my mother's word. Please save me from any damage and harm that was caused to my body.

I will just lock myself in my room to recover for a few days, then go on with life as normally as possible.

Renee

Renee was just lying there in bed next to her husband, Tommy, hoping he would not wake up and try anything this morning. She hated the thought of sex with him, and for the last ten years, she wished daily that she had not fallen into the pressure of marriage only because of the success of the person she was dating at the time. Sometimes people only see the dollar signs someone can add to their bank account and not the value someone can add to your life. Her mom and her sisters were such ladies. They preached to their female cousins, "You are the prize, so he will have to pay." Renee shuddered at the thought of them. All of them were estranged. She could not remember the last time she spoke to her mother, and although she wanted to feel a pang of guilt or even loss, no such feeling came over her. Again, she wondered if the words her husband mumbled about her last night were true: "She was a rigidly cold woman."

She did not think the words were meant for her ears, but she heard them nonetheless. He was on the phone with someone in their home office. Renee was late coming home from work as usual, and as she came in the room…

"Yea, Renee is late as usual. I sometimes wonder if I have to go to her job just to see her face." Her husband laughed at his joke and listened to the person on the other end for a bit.

"Man, that's not all I feel. She never wants to do anything. Never wants to go anywhere. It is as if her life is consumed by work and moving up, and I am just an inconvenience or something."

He went silent again as Renee waited by the door. Her heart beat in her ears, and she could feel her chest moving, despite her desire to calm her racing pulse. She was inept to stop the fast-moving train that easy listening had her riding on. What did he think of her? Was he still in love with her? Did he want to be with her?

Three years ago, Renee had realized that she had never loved him the way he seemed to love her. She had made sure to take on the role as the perfect wife and to fulfill that role, but she was apparently failing at the ability to submit and put her husband's needs first. Her career was everything, and she had worked so hard toward it.

"I'm a bad, bad chick" the song lyrics played in the background as Renee drove her late-modeled vehicle into the parking lot. Once again, she was the first to arrive at work, and this was the way she preferred it. She craved the silence of the office before people showed up, when she would be forced to smile and pretend to be happy. She left her husband at home again, as he was not due to work at the hospital for another three hours, but she was suffocating in that house! Yes, the house was large, and yes, it had all the modern amenities that any woman could want, but Renee was not happy in that house. It screamed, "Money, money, money, moonneeey," like the song, but it was empty of love.

Renee exited the car, walked confidently up to the office doors, then used her keycard to enter. As she walked, her four-inch Milano Blahnik shoes clicked against the floor. She smiled at the sound. She had bought these shoes two weeks ago at Saks, and for a brief moment, she felt good. But, like all the other times, buying things did not complete her or replace the hole she felt in her chest every night and all through the day. Work! Work made her feel important and fulfilled, but at some point, she had to leave the office and return home.

Entering her office on the fourth floor, she paused at the door and scanned the office with the eyes of someone seeing it for the first time.

She noticed the sofa, smiling. It had cost her upwards of fifteen thousand dollars, and she still marveled that with her history, she could afford something so extravagant. She knew that most people would not look at the sofa and think fifteen thousand dollars, but knowing that it cost that much made it just that special to her. The conference table in the middle of the floor was a must as well, and the seven chairs that circled the table were also top of the line. These nice things brought Renee joy, but that joy did not last. That joy did not stay with her.

"Happy Feelings" played, Renee's ring tone that signaled her husband was calling. He must have woken up and realized she was gone. What did he want? She answered...

"Good morning, sweetie," she said, not feeling the sugary word as it fell from her lips.

"Babe, you left early again this morning? I thought you and I would have time to talk."

Darn, she thought, *I did mention going into work later this morning, but damn, why stay in the bed next to someone you can't stand?*

"Oh, sweetheart, I am just running here quickly to handle something, and I will be right back home."

"You couldn't handle that from your home office?" Her husband was whining, and she could not stand that mess.

Renee was getting annoyed, and in a minute, it would become difficult to hide her annoyance from her husband. "Now, Tommy, you know some things are classified. and it is better handled at the office."

"But you drove for forty-five minutes from the house. You will spend about an hour at the office and then drive that same amount of time back. I will be late getting to the hospital waiting for you to come home so we can talk."

"So, Tommy, are you saying that your job is more important than mine? Because you are okay with me getting in to work late, but you are complaining about the time you will have to be late. I don't recall a surgery on your schedule today."

Renee sat behind her desk, waiting for his next words. They would be the last ones she heard from him, and he had no idea of their impact.

Renee was a vice president of operations at a notable hospital. She was the first minority in that position, and she demonstrated poised professionalism and progression within months of her role. She was always happy and positive, bringing the sunshine to the organization on a rainy day. Most of the staff relied on her smile to get them through the day. She accepted her role as it came and played it well. Her empathy and compassion resonated through the organization like no other. In reality, there was truly not another administrator of her cantor. It was like God had placed Renee in that position to service patients and employees as needed.

The organization released a press release of Renee's passing, which shocked everyone. Renee did not appear to have any physical ailments. She was middle-aged, very active, and in shape. She was a woman of God and a listening ear to most, and her words of wisdom and inspiration ranged amongst many, making realizing and accepting her death even harder. She was beautiful and had the most beautiful smile. Her death was associated with an accidental overdose.

She showed many signs of sadness; however, these were not "typical" signs. She was always smiling and spewing the "good news." Every day, she hid behind a beat face and fierce wardrobe. She knew how to cope in any situation of danger or defeat. For most, this is an indication of a strong, God-fearing woman who had favor. All this was true, except Renee also had a hidden secret.

Renee suffered in silence with a level of depression that took her out, partially because she was seen as the strong one, the caretaker, the educated sister, the successful aunt who opted to have a career over motherhood, the positive and inspirational friend with the best advice, the leader, the organizer, and much more. She was known for her forty-thousand-plus square foot house, with a G Wagon, a Bentley, and a

Maserati in the garage. Even though she was the donor of many organizations and a board member to multiple non-profits, the question still resonated: how could she have an accidental overdose? Was it really suicide? Renee had been blessed with an amazing life. How could she not be happy?

Most were unaware of Renee's past, which she worked hard to ensure did not define her. For many years, her secret had been safe between herself, her psychiatrist, and journals. She often toggled with why God had allowed certain tragedies to happen to her, but she was not ready to share her past for fear of judgement. At a young age, she learned to put a smile on her face and increase her energy and enthusiasm so that no one would realize that a tragedy was taking place. Although she had plenty of tangible items, Renee was still lonely. Yet how could one be lonely with a thriving career, a busy schedule, and a marriage to a prominent plastic surgeon?

> "Those who plant only for their own benefit will harvest devastation from their selfishness, but those who plant for the benefit of the Spirit will harvest eternal life from the Spirit." Galatians 6:8(CEB)"

Stacy

Dinner was ready, and Stacy still had ten minutes on the timer. Damn, she was good! She patted herself on her back and looked over the counter into the dining room, where her three children sat around the table, completing their homework assignments. She smiled to herself. Her home was her pride and joy. She took a gratifying breathe as she slowly walked over toward the table where her children quietly worked. This was their routine, for they knew that in order to play outside after dinner or to even look at television, homework had to come first. She noticed that, on some Monday nights, the kids tried to complete some of Tuesday night's homework as well. Stacy guessed that this was because they had homework sheets for the week and some teachers were able to plan ahead. Her babies were ahead of the game.

"How are you all coming along? Do you need my help with anything?" She quickened her pace just in case, but she reached the table.

"I'm done, Ma, but you can check it to see if I have it right," Stacy's oldest Charles said, looking up at her with a smile. He was an overachiever, and Stacy was proud of him. He was a promising engineer always tinkering with this and that, hoping to get something just right—perfect, actually. She sighed, thinking, *soon he will be out of the house and on to college. Child one gone, check!*

"Let me take a look."

"I'm done too, Mom!"

"Me too!"

She looked around the table, and the three children were all closing their books and clearing the table. "Wait, fellas. I still need to see what you did."

"Well, you already have mine in your hand."

"Here's mine."

"Uh, here," her middle child quickly handed her his paper and headed for his room, book bag slung over his shoulder as he ran up the stairs.

"Joseph!" Stacy smiled as she called him back to the dining room. "Son, why didn't you ask for help?" He walked slowly back to her.

"I don't know, Mom," he shrugged.

She glanced over at her kitchen timer. She had seven minutes before dinner was supposed to be on the table. Mind you, this was her own self-proposed time, but it was the schedule. "Sit down, son." She said to Joseph. "Sam, Charles, go find something to do until it is time for dinner. Charles, this is your week for dishes, Sam, your trash week." Her other two sons nodded and walked up the stairs as she began assisting Joseph with his math homework.

Stacy had been a math whiz in school, so much so, she was offered a math scholarship to MIT. The middle school math problems were easy enough for her to explain, and Joseph was well on his way correcting the assigned problems when the side door opened. Stacy looked over at the timer. *Damn it!* It was ten minutes past the dinner time, and the table was not set. "Uh, Charles, Sam!" she shouted so she could be heard upstairs. "Wash your hands for dinner."

"Thanks, Mom, that was easy after you explained it," Joseph said, blushing. Stacy smiled down at him.

"Where's dinner? I wanted to get home in time to eat with the family tonight." Charles Jr. sat his briefcase on the floor next to the door and took off his suit coat. He scanned to dining room table and looked up at his wife expectedly.

She sighed. "Joseph was having trouble with his math, so I sat down to help him. Don't worry, dinner is already done in the kitchen. I just need to set the table."

He nodded, but tried to think of something to rush along this process. "Uh, Joseph, set the table for everybody, but wash your hands first." He picked up his briefcase and walked to their master suite on the first floor of the house. Stacy watched him walk away without a gesture for a kiss. "Good to see you too, honey," she mumbled to herself.

Feeling dejected, she walked back into the kitchen. Where was her kiss hello? She completed the tasks of setting the table and getting the food out to the dining room. As everyone sat down, her husband looked over at her. "Where are the drinks?"

Slowly, she turned toward her husband. "Usually the boys get their own drinks and bring them to the table," she explained. Her children reached for their glasses. Charles grabbed his and his mother's, and Joseph took his and his father's off the table. Sam had only his glass in his hands, and they all walked to the kitchen. "Tell them what you would like to drink," Stacy instructed her husband.

"Oh, uh, tea is fine."

She nodded. "Your father would prefer tea, C-Three," She called out to her oldest. This is what she called Charles when his father was around to distinguish them.

Joseph came back first and sat his mother's glass on the table, then sat down in the chair.

Do you remember growing up as a little girl, playing with dolls, sewing doll clothes, cooking in the Easy Bake oven, pretending to be a mother and a wife? I do, and so did Stacy. Stacy was the epitome of stay-at-home wife and mother. Unknowingly, the world prepares us for that role at an early age; we are so prepared that we think nurturing, cooking, and cleaning are naturally second nature, when we have actually been studying and fixating on this behavior for years.

Stacy

Stacy, a mom of four and a loving wife of fifteen years, loved to be needed. She studied the ways of Julia and Martha to keep things new and fresh for her family. She was phenomenal at her roles of mother and wife. Her efforts, however, often went unnoticed, but that only pushed her to try to satisfy her family even more. Her husband would often come home in an unruly mood. Stacy would have his whisky ready, a listening ear for venting, dinner prepared, a bath drawn, and his television pre-set in the den. Usually, by the time he came home, the kids had completed their homework and dinner and had settled into bed. In the evenings, her husband had her to himself, and during the day, the kids had her to themselves. When did Stacy have her to herself?

Stacy had the purest heart and served her family effortlessly for fear of messing up or being left. She wanted to be seen as more than the caretaker, but she was unsure of her other talents. In the past, she had witnessed her dad leave her mom, for reasons she was unsure of, but Stacy could only assume that her mom had not been domestic enough. Her mom had been a nurse and had often worked long hours, leaving Stacy to assist with household duties. Her dad was a banker, so his days were pretty routine, which led to a feeling of resentment or loneliness toward his wife. Stacy's dad often took his feelings out on Stacy. Although Stacy just wanted love and approval, her duties went unnoticed, and her dad eventually left their family. Stacy clearly saw differently for her own future. She put her all into her family, never intending on a career of her own. However, the love was still missing. The kids assumed their mom was just being a mom, and her husband was so involved in himself that he didn't even realize Stacy was always two steps ahead of his needs and wants. Eventually, darkness set in for Stacy. She continued to serve her family, but with no sense of fulfillment; she was now filled with dismay.

> "That's how husbands ought to love their wives—in the same way as they do their own bodies. Anyone who loves his wife loves himself." Ephesians 5:28(CEB)

Stacy had always looked for love from others. Once her dad abandoned her and her mom became unavailable due to committing to her career, Stacy was determined to make the best of her own family, but all she felt was a sense of abandonment and a lack of appreciation and love. Individuals often put their needs first, even if sometimes unintentionally, which is why we shouldn't look for validation and love in man. God is forever, and unlike man, His character never changes.

> "For do I now persuade men, or God? Or do I seek to please men? For if I yet pleased men, I should not be the servant of Christ." Galatians 1:10(CEB)

In order to find happiness, Stacy began to self-cope. She would take a drink to take the edge off. She would take a drink to feel better about scorching her family's dinner. She would take a drink to feel less lonely. She would take a drink until one day, her coping turned into a real addiction. Stacy's issues started with lack of validation from a man.

Diana

Why does it seem that your hard work is wasted? The sacrifices you made, the experiences you granted and introduced, the tangible wants and needs you provided, were they all a waste? I often ask myself, what could I have done differently to resort with a different outcome? I thought I was doing my best…I gave my child time, love, money, things I was never given while growing up. I worked hard and sacrificed a lot of personal desires, trips, and cosmetic offerings to ensure I provided a quality life for my child. I've put extra thought and love into everything I've done, although my daughter thought my love was so tough and perhaps overbearing. I made sure she had college savings, even though this left me hundreds of thousands of dollars in debt. I even bought real-estate properties that I left for her once they were paid out. As a child, I enrolled her in every sport, dance class, acting and modeling school, speech and debate course, along with etiquette and debutant programs to assist her in becoming the best woman she could be. At the time, it seemed like overkill, but you don't know what you can do, what you like to do, or what may peak your interest unless you've tried it. Throughout my daughter's childhood, every two years, the family traveled to major fun resorts, then during her young adulthood, we introduced her to Italy, Paris, France, and Hawaii. She was very involved in the church; for me, knowing God and knowing Him for herself was very important to teach her. I know that without Him, I could not have provided any of these opportunities for her.

No, I wasn't a single mother. My husband, her father, was in the picture, but the problem is that I was able to control everything in the best interest of our daughter. He gratuitously allowed me to, but he would step up at times when my daughter felt I was being "too much" or "too extra." I love my husband because he loves me dearly; he accepts my accomplishments, although he is extremely accomplished himself. He was born into his money and knew I wasn't, but he also understood that I didn't marry him for his. In fact, it took me five years to finally go on a first date with him. My husband knew I was not going to have a daughter who had to struggle as long as I was alive.

My daughter had a two-parent home in a gated community, a busy schedule, limited rules, and a strong-headed mother, but our home was still pretty liberal—free and open to self-expression. My husband was a lawyer turned judge—hint at speech and debate classes—and we hoped she would follow in one of our footsteps. Most definitely, she ended up in his field, just on the wrong side. I, myself, started off in healthcare and education, but I found more fulfillment in my own consulting firm. The money in this was also great, as was the added flexibility of creating how busy I wanted to be or not to be, especially with my love of traveling.

Danielle chose to find her own happiness and not her mother's plan for her life. The love of a man, his attention, to be defiant? It was definitely not for the money. How did he get off? He was the cause of her demise, for he surely introduced her to the drug world. Hooked on heroin at twenty-seven. "Only a dab will do you" is an old but true saying. When she met Dave, Danielle was a nurse, actually, a nurse practitioner. Dave was a patient of hers who stole her heart. How did a gunshot victim in ICU steal Danielle's heart? Her mother, Diana, is still waiting on an answer for that. In fact, Danielle's whole village is wondering and at a loss for words.

After being shot in a drive-by twenty-seven times, Dave fully recovered. He was left lifeless in his car at a red light, and after sixteen surgeries, fifty blood transfusions, and being comatose, he rose like Jesus from the grave—not actually, but damn, Diana is still trying to figure out how he fully recovered and swept her baby girl, Danielle, off her feet. Once David was released from the hospital and the case was closed on his shooting, Danielle left her parents' estate and moved in with him. David had a nice home in a great subdivision as well, but the means through which he reached his level of success was questionable to Danielle's parents. Of course, being a target in a shootout didn't help the case, along with no witnesses in sight, especially when the shooting took place at a super busy intersection. Anyway, Danielle found love, fell in love, and nothing her overpowering mother could say would change her mind on moving in with Dave, with hopes of marriage and kids.

Danielle used to visit her parents every two weeks for dinner and conversation, and those weeks later turned into months. Diana became concerned during this time and she checked on Danielle while at lunch one day. Danielle just explained to her that between work and school, and with the addition of playing wifey, her schedule was consumed. Danielle then decided to open up about how she had a recent miscarriage and was just exhausted. Her mom explained that her heavy load may just be stressful, and it might not be a part of the plan at this current moment. Diana told her she should just finish her doctoral program. Danielle agreed and went back to work.

While shopping, Diana bumped into Danielle's childhood friend, who asked Diana, in a surprised yet concerned voice, "How you have been?"

"Great! Never better," Diana replied.

The young lady explained that she hadn't spoken to Danielle in months, and when they caught up over the phone, Danielle mentioned that both of her parents had fallen ill, and along with work and school, life had just become overwhelming. Danielle then mentioned to her friend, that these difficulties were the primary reasons why she sat out of school the following semester. Diana was shocked, but not wanting to make Danielle out to be a liar, she went along with it. Once she left the friend, she immediately called Danielle. Of course, there was no answer, so she was familiar with her excuse of being at work. Diana had to drop off some information to a few medical clients, so she went to the hospital, hoping to see Danielle and have lunch to catch up, especially after hearing that she was a part of her fabrication in being MIA. Anyway, after Diana could not find Danielle in her usual areas, she bumped into an old friend of Danielle who was a nurse and asked if she had seen Danielle or could call scheduling to see who the charge nurse was; it was an emergency. The nurse told Diana that Danielle hadn't been working there in a month or longer. She was under investigation for medication fraud and suspended, but she decided to quit. Diana was shocked, confused, and in dismay, she just didn't understand why...well, other than David entering her life.

Diana drove to David's house, but security wouldn't let her in, and of course, when she called for entry, no one answered her number. She became even more worried, especially because she did not know the current situation of her daughter after learning that she was living a lie, a false life that had led her astray from her family, friends, and career. For four hours, Diana camped out on the road that led into the estate where Danielle was living, until she decided to leave. Feeling a loss of emotions, a loss of words, and full of worry as fear and confusion set in, all Diana could do was pray to God that Danielle was safe from all harm, that she was in her right mind, and that she would contact her soon. Then Diana drove home in silence, trying to understand where she went wrong and what her daughter had gotten herself into.

Once a day, Diana called David and Danielle's line and passed around their subdivision every other day. Still no answer, no contact, no message saying Danielle was alright and there was no need to worry.

After four months, prayer was all Diana could do; she stopped passing around David's home and began to call less. Diana reported Danielle missing and in harm, but the detectives were able to reach Danielle, who told them that she was not missing or in harm's way. So the detective notified Diana of her well-being. At that point, Diana let Danielle be.

One day, Diana was home watching *Cops and Cases,* and this season was filmed in her city. Lord behold, guess who was on the show...yes, David. He had been arrested for a murder charge during a drug bust. Diana searched the police registry for Danielle, but nothing populated. She then searched for David and found several charges. After some further research, she saw an arrest address that took place six months ago, so she decided to go to the address to find out if anyone knew Danielle or David. She wasn't scared and felt it was worth the risk. When she pulled up to the house, she saw that it was a true crack or trap house, straight from the movies or rap videos. Knock, knock, knock...no one answered. She heard movement, then peeked down the side of the house and knocked harder; a doorbell could not be found.

Diana was so desperate for answers that she went and opened the door. In the home, several people were present, but they were stretched out throughout the rooms on the floor, laying lifeless, dead to the world, faint, discolored, bruised, just overwhelmingly in need of help. She went through each room searching for answers, not really wanting Danielle to be there, but hoping she was there to end the search. Diana finally made it to the last room of the house, where two ladies were in the corner, hugging each other. As she approached them and rolled them over, tears filled her eyes, her heart sank deeper, and she broke down because she had come to the end of the road with no answers...and Danielle was not there.

Another month passed, and Diana decided to do another search through the jail database. She searched local and statewide, but nothing populated. She then decided to pay a visit to David to see if he was willing to offer some information since he was locked up. David denied her visit. One day, Diana decided to camp out in the parking lot of the jail on visitation day, and bam! She noticed a lady who resembled her daughter.

She waited patiently for the lady to return to her car and followed her home. The neighborhood was the same one that Diana had searched. After watching Danielle's mannerisms from afar as she hung out on a porch surrounded by other males, Diana gathered strength and approached Danielle in a calm manner. Nervous and scared, but wanting to not scare her away, Diana made her way to the steps, spoke to everyone, and asked Danielle if she could come down the stairs for a moment to talk to her. The guys surrounded Diana, as if they were Danielle's bodyguards. Diana asked the guys to step back and respect her space, then she boldly told them, "I need to speak with my daughter."

Danielle stood up and asked Diane to please leave. "Not without speaking to you," Diana responded. Danielle said she didn't want her to see her like that and she would call her later, but Diana knew that was a lie because she has not heard from Danielle in almost a year. As the guys approached Diana to force her to move, Diana resisted and told Danielle that she would come up there since Danielle refused to come down the stairs. The men started to push Diana toward the street, even roughing her up a bit. Diana pleaded for Danielle to just talk to her, so Danielle asked the guys to stop and made her way to the sidewalk. Diana hugged her, kissed her forehead, and checked her body for visible bruises or wounds. Danielle appeared to be intact, her skin seemed to have aged, and her eyes looked a bit swollen from exhaustion or crying. Diana asked how she was doing. "Everything is fine, Mom," Danielle said.

"Are you safe?" Diana asked.

"Yes," Danielle answered.

"Then are you happy living this lifestyle, Danielle?"

"What lifestyle you are referencing?" Danielle asked.

Diana answered, "The streets…it appears that you have chosen the streets, a man that's in jail, and to be surrounded by thugs instead of a loving family and friends."

Diana then went on a rant about the things she had sacrificed to provide the perfect life and world for Danielle, who threw it all away and abandoned everything and everyone in a matter of months for David.

Danielle interrupted, saying, "This is why—your constant reminder of what you sacrificed, the pressure you put on me not to fail at life, the notion that I had to be perfect so I didn't let you or the family down, the lack of love and nurturing provided, and the happy facade that was created to keep Daddy's name perfect in the community. That's why I disappeared, abandoned my fake family and friends, and hung up the career I never wanted. It wasn't me. I chose David and the streets, because they saw me for me. David allowed me to be me. He loved the true me. He saw right through the scrubs at the hospital and knew that I was hiding behind a false identity that I had adopted to please you. Being myself, the ratchet, street person that you may think is below our family's standards, is who I truly enjoy being. It was depressing studying for hours to ensure I met your dreams, not mine. I never wanted to work in healthcare, nor in law. I never even considered being a teacher. I would be simply okay with a standard job as a cashier or housekeeper and coming home to a happy family that I can enjoy. Not an empty dinner table or a large home that is isolated because everyone is still working."

Danielle then told Diana that if she could not accept the lifestyle that she was living, then she should leave and never return. She explained that David had made his own trouble and bed for himself, and he was paying for it. She loved David regardless because of how he treated her, how he loved her back, and how he did not put too many expectations on her. Diana was still puzzled by it all, explaining that she only wanted the best for her daughter. Danielle told Diana that this was best for her. Diana said that was the dumbest thing she had ever heard and asked Danielle how she could be happy living like this. She told Danielle that she was an embarrassment and disgrace to the family and that she needed to leave with her now, or else she would call the police to come to that drug house.

Danielle eyes filled up with tears. "You didn't hear a word I said," she replied to her mother. She asked Diana to leave and never comeback, then went inside the house. Diana yelled for Danielle to come back outside, but she never did. Diana eventually left and never returned.

Parents should not expect their children to do exactly as they desire. As much as we as parents hope and dream, our children will have minds of their own. They will not do what we want all the time, and as parents we have to know that our faith in God and his love will cover our children in all of their decisions.

> "The reward of humility and the fear of the LORD is wealth, honor, and life." Proverbs 22:4(CEB)

Vanessa

Have you ever judged someone for being a whore, fast, or a jezebel? Have you ever envied someone for their free-spirited ways or their ability to date multiple men? Can you be honest and agree that you have actually lived vicariously through someone like this, but due to the stigma people hold against a female serial dater, you judged her as well?

Vanessa was young and beautiful, obsessed with the thought of love. She wanted to feel love at all times. Men approached her all the time, and she would date them and even have sex with them, then find a reason to drop them. She embraced her sexuality and often bragged about her techniques. She admitted that her sex drive was very high and that she didn't mind one-night stands. Still, Vanessa often complained about being single and lonely. How could a person who was constantly dating feel single and alone?

At times, Vanessa was fighting the wrong urge. Sex was her addiction. Every orgasm made her feel loved, and she coupled sex and love together. In reality, she was afraid of commitment and the hurt that came with falling in love. She wanted to marry one day, but she couldn't understand why she hadn't found her Boaz. Once a relationship began to get routine, Vanessa found a reason to drop the guy. Of course, that sexual urge would return and needed to be fulfilled. She was on to the next guy.

Most saw Vanessa's lifestyle as free or risky. Vanessa needed to figure out the underlying problem that made her lust for sex in order to fill the missing piece of love. One day, a friend made her realize that her past abandonment and daddy issues had gotten in the way of her ability to settle down. Once Vanessa accepted that she was her own problem, she began to work on herself.

> "No temptation has overtaken you except what is common to mankind. And God is faithful; he will not let you be tempted beyond what you can bear. But when you are tempted, he will also provide a way out so that you can endure it." 1 Corinthians 7:13-15(CEB)

Finally, Vanessa found love and settled down. She was happy with the attention her man provided and the constant orgasms, and that he was respectful and supportive of her career, while also very good looking. They would make beautiful kids together. Once engaged, Vanessa knew sex was an addiction of hers and wanted to abstain from it until after the wedding, to make things right with God and to show gratefulness for finding her Boaz. They married, moved in together, and soon became pregnant. They were living the American dream. One evening, Vanessa's doctor asked that she came in to review her prenatal test. She was then informed that her HIV test was positive. She went through a range of emotions because she had finally committed, settled for love, trusted her husband, prayed for him, and fasted and abstained from sex to contract HIV from him.

A hormonal, enraged Vanessa went home and confronted her husband. Shocked and worried, he told her that she was the second person he had ever been with and scheduled an appointment to get tested. He tested negative, and it appeared that Vanessa contracted HIV prior to her marriage of three months.

> "Stolen water is sweet; food eaten in secret is pleasant." Proverbs 9:17(CEB)

Jamie

Have you ever wondered how a person could be so "green" to common situations? So judgmental yet so positive and happy in the same breath? Well, Jamie was a ray of sunshine 24/7. She didn't understand poverty, depression, lack of motivation, nothing that consisted of being denied or turned away. Jamie was blessed to have two loving and supportive parents who paid her way through college, purchased her first car, and placed a down payment on a condo in the city for her. Jamie's dad got her an internship at one of the top financial firms, which later hired her for an executive position after she obtained her MBA.

She had a few friends, but she often struggled with her friendships yet never understood why. She felt she offered opinions and tips on having a successful life such as hers and constantly preached about the power of prayer. Jamie was very open and appreciative of the fact that God showed her plenty of favor, and she was not shy about it. However, her lack of empathy toward her friends' financial situations and indications of their lack of faith drew a wedge in her relationships. She made it hard for friends to vent to her, so although she found herself progressing in life, she was progressing alone.

Jamie developed the idea that everyone was jealous of her success. She didn't understand why her friends were consumed in student loan debt, why they didn't own property before thirty, why they had to be financially responsible for their sick parents, or why her best friend settled for a job that she was unhappy with. She didn't understand why her friends couldn't just pick up and fly to Dubai. Jamie was very sheltered, closed-minded, unknowingly selfish, and judgmental, and she lacked empathy for others. She constantly praised God for her come ups, but she looked down at the homeless and rarely volunteered to help those less fortunate than her. In her head, she believed she had accomplished it all on her own.

> "Live in harmony with one another. Do not be proud, but be willing to associate with people of low position. Do not be conceited. Do not repay anyone evil for evil. Be careful to do what is right in the eyes of everyone. If it is possible, as far as it depends on you, live at peace with everyone." Romans 12:16-18(CEB)

Jamie later married an executive from her firm. They had the perfect wedding, bought the perfect house, and began living a lavish dream. Still, Jamie found herself a bit lonely; most of her friends became estranged or tied up with their own lives and left Jamie out because of her lack of understanding. On the outside, Jamie kept the appearance that everything was perfect, but at home, she felt like a failure.

Her husband, Tom, didn't understand why she couldn't do something as simple as conceive a child. They had been trying for five years, and Jamie had never gotten pregnant, something most of her friends had already accomplished. Motherhood was one thing she was behind on. Tom, an investment banker, was a risk taker; he had pooled their assets together and invested in some stock that crashed, causing them to lose everything. Jamie began to lose faith in God just because she began to encounter real-life situations. Instead of continuing to praise God as she had done before, she started to question and resent Him.

She started to fuss and question God and her husband daily, saying, "I prayed for you, a savior, a king, someone who was the total opposite of my friends' husbands. I prayed for a man who would love me unconditionally, want me, and need me, someone who cherished and appreciated me. God blessed me with you. You became my husband. It was years before I allowed you to be the one. I wanted to make sure we were right for each other. Sometimes it's hard to tell when God is speaking to you or if it's your inner self.

"In the beginning, you chased me, and I ran." Jamie often thought she was better and kind of enjoyed the chasing. "You didn't give up; you became very innovative in tracking me down and winning me over. I felt the attraction you had for me. I had witnessed a lot of women who were lost and used to being abused, so I was willing to be reassured of the positive attention you showed me. You made your presence known in my life. You helped and supported me during the toughest situation I had experienced, and that's when I let my guard down and gave myself to you. My choice, no forceful invitation. Although we both were in it for the friendship and the sex, we grew on each other fast. Next, we were in a relationship.

During our college years, our love was so fresh. We were happy, and we sacrificed our life to see each other, to be with each other, to lie up against one and another, even if it was just for twenty minutes. You were the first person who I felt actually loved me for me, not what I could do for them. You treated me well, spoiled me, respected me, nurtured me, supported me, and accepted me, flaws and all. You even accepted my family and all of their stern beliefs. At one time, you enjoyed their company and thought their actions were full of hilarity and respected them in a dignified manner. Years of dating finally led to marriage, and after a very rocky year with career changes, I wasn't even sure if we would make it to that point. I wanted you and was very eager to get what I wanted, so guess what? It happened. I now wonder if that was a message from God to not enter marriage. At times, we ignore signs to get what we want, then we feel the regret later. Perhaps it was just the devil trying to step in my path to happiness. Everything has been upside down since year five.

After ten years of being in each other lives and five years of marriage, I often tell myself and God, 'This is not what I asked for.' You changed from the guy whom I had once felt safe with. You once loved me; now that feeling is gone. You once cherished me and respected me, but now I am just your servant and arm candy. You have placed all of my dreams on the backburner; everything I want to do is second to the desires of others. Our hugs and kisses have turned into stares and fist fights. I never thought I would be the one to say, 'You got one more time to hit me.' You often make me feel like my value and self-worth have bottomed out, making me push harder to be perfect. Of course, I know that no one is perfect, but I have still strived to be the perfect wife, daughter, friend, and career woman, but I could never reach that feeling of accomplishment. No matter how much gratitude I received from others, you had a way of making me feel like I still was not doing enough or I was wrong for doing anything at all.

As I sit in your presence with a slight, graceful smile, I wonder how I got to this place in my life. I often think I might feel less empty if I would have made a better selection. I thought carefully during the process of determining who I would spend my future with, yet I now feel alone, dissatisfied, and unhappy. I play the role of a happy wife, I serve my king gracefully, I care for my home without complaint or remorse, but then, when no one is around, I fall into deep sorrow. To mask to pain I keep inside, I just motion through the years heavily medicated. I dare not tell anyone, not even a medical professional, after deeming and condemning so many others for this feeling.

"I often wonder; how did I get here?" I know my husband cares for me, to the point where he becomes overbearing. Many have said they would kill to have a person care for them so much, but I feel smothered. Is that the character of a good man, and am I just being ungrateful? I never expressed any down points, abuse, or illnesses of my life or marriage, so they are only looking inside. The fact that I want to run into hiding actually frightens me. My husband wants me all to himself, isolated from friends and family. He wants to be alone with me and wishes for the kids I cannot give him. Interactions with anyone else are rare. Of course, I comply. I'm the faithful wife trying to make her marriage work. After all, I am living the great life that my parents had always told me I must have. I own more things than my parents did, and they were very accomplished. Now, I have my own things they only saw in their dreams, and it's all due to my husband. But again, why am I still empty?

The overbearing makes me reflect on the days of slavery or women's suffrage, when permission was needed to make a move. I am a grown woman who takes care of my home, domestically and financially, but my king doesn't treat me as his queen; instead, I am his personal slave, since I cannot conceive a child. My man believes that his actions are out of pure love and that he has great intentions. However, I feel trapped, as my purpose of self is drifting down the sideline. My dominance and strong character are submitting to my husband's behavior, abuse, and misleading guidance, and I am slowly dying inside because I feel empty. The I-love-yous and honey-you-are-so-beautifuls do not equate to the freedom one holds to make decisions in their household. I love my husband dearly, but I have this range of hate at the same time. What to do? It switches from day to day. I'm afraid to tell anyone because of the opinions that may be true, so I hide, I lay inside, and I am truly mentally exhausted from the everyday worry of doing what pleases my husband.

Due to the constant reminder of all the things I come from, my heart continues to ache. I feel heartless and have developed hatred because my success to overcome the misfits in my family is overlooked and our relationship and decisions are based on their mishaps. The constant reminders pain me and mentally set me back. My husband makes me feel that everything we currently have is his doing, and I somewhat get brain washed into thinking that, until I reassure myself that I am the key to my own success and that I have played a big part in our combined success, if not more. What I never understood was that fact that a woman must submit to man, stroke his ego, and push and support him in his dreams, but a woman must also ignore a man's behavior when he degrades her and fails to support her.

My mind is constantly filled with the struggle and thoughts about how and why I often feel broken, falling into pieces, my heart shattered, my head all over the place. Excessive hormones must still be present throughout my body; I'm happy one week and depressed the next, but I will push harder. What else am I supposed to do? As black women, we are told we must be strong and pick up the pieces when times are hard. We must put on a smile, not letting anyone in on our problems but God. That's one thing I am good at—faking it—my happiness, that is—while accomplishing goals and catering and ministering to others. As exhaustion sets in, anxiety appears, depression takes over, and my coffee cup and energy drinks become my savior. Sorry, God, but I just can't push myself anymore, and I think I lost You along the way. Circular yellow pills, tiny peach pills, and an occasional white pill with blue dots become my secret passage to pushing through it all with a smile.

As time went on, life became much easier. My husband calmed down, and I felt that he once again loved me, cherished me, and respected me like the old days. I was in love with the thought and feeling of someone loving me. As a child, I was told that this was the type of man I wanted or was supposed to have, and I always longed for that lost love but managed to mask it well. So, as you can see, this routine is easy for me to cycle into. I think I purposely did things to make my husband snap because having that loving, caring person was not my norm; it appeared to be smothering at times. At first, I didn't mind the snapping because I knew he loved me, and he was committed and was always there and didn't mean it, until the love was lost and his commitment and thoughtfulness became stalkerish. Well, I enjoyed the bit of peace that welcomed its way back. I was able to reduce the fakeness for a while, to unveil and remove the mask. From the outside, everyone looking in wished they had my lifestyle. A very close friend would always say, 'At least he cares about you and looks for you.' Another drilled on the fact that he chased me to marry me, and she is still looking to marry. My mom always looked at what he buys me, or should I say, used to buy me."

Jaime judged others not knowing that she would face trials herself. We should not look down on others and their situations because we do not know what God will have us experience. As Jaime pours out her heart, we see her pain and know she is not fulfilled. She thought being a wife and mother would be enough, but God saw fit to show her she needed God too. When we are feeling lost and confused, we should seek God. Listening for his voice can help us through.

> "But he said to me, 'My grace is sufficient for you, for my power is made perfect in weakness.' Therefore, I will boast all the more gladly about my weaknesses, so that Christ's power may rest on me. That is why, for Christ's sake, I delight in weaknesses, in insults, in hardships, in persecutions, in difficulties. For when I am weak, then I am strong." 2 Corinthians 12:9-10(CEB)

Amanda

*H*old up, the idea was to save money and lose weight in the process, so was I supposed to cook four pieces of chicken and eat it in one sitting? Has gluttony taken over my life, or was it just pure satisfaction of the love of chicken? Amanda stood at the stove looking down at the now half-empty pan that should have been filled with chicken, knowing that the amount was supposed to have lasted her four days. The idea was to cut down on the amount she ate, that she would eat more vegetables to make her meal. As she stared at the pan longer, lo and behold, just like she knew would happen, she had eaten four large thighs and was now feeling guilty. No one else was in the house with her, but she felt as if eyes raked all over her body, judging her as if she was pathetic and undesirable. She knew this was her own judgement of herself, and it hurt her to know that she had failed again. She was not stressed or overwhelmed like other people claimed they were when they overate, but in her mind, there was food, and so she ate her fill.

She sighed and pulled out the storage containers from the bottom cabinet on the left of the stove. "I failed again," she said out loud. Another feeling just as dark as failure overcame her as she looked around her kitchen. She did not want to be in there. There were not many dishes because it was just her at the house, but while looking around at the countertops, the thought of washing dishes seemed just as daunting a task as losing the fifty-five pounds she needed to get off her body in order to be "healthier."

She walked into her living room and plopped down on her plush grey sofa, and her eyes wandered to the television. Some Lifetime movie played as another woman "overcame" some man hurting her. *Humph, did the story ever change? It was either that or two people falling in love after some impossible meeting. It was instant, and they knew they were to be together forever.* She stuck her tongue out at the television and made a childish sound. Whatever! There was never anybody just living life! What the hell did she know about living life to judge? Okay, so maybe she was being too dramatic and oversimplifying the movies on Lifetime.

Disgusted again with her thoughts, she turned on her favorite movie, *Harry Potter and the Sorcerer's Stone*. She smiled as she watched again as a young Harry was rescued from his awful aunt and uncle. She chuckled to herself that she could watch this fantasy and not the Lifetime Channel.

The time on the cable box read ten o'clock, and she needed to be up for work at five, so it was time to shower and get in bed. She briefly thought about stepping on the treadmill for ten minutes to work off all of that chicken but scoffed at the thought.

The next day, Amanda stood in the employee lounge of her office building, daydreaming of the new Popeye's chicken sandwich.

"What're you doing? What's wrong with you?"

Amanda turned slowly and made a smile appear on her face. She was guilty of thinking about food, again. She looked up at her closest friend at work, Morris. "Hey, Morris, I am out of it this morning. How are you?"

Morris stopped and stared at her. Pausing before he spoke, he shook his head. "I am not sure how to say this." Amanda slowly leaned her head to the side and waited, unsure of what he would say.

He reached out his arm and lay his head on her shoulder. He took a deep breath. "So, I know you are struggling with something. Wait, hear me out before you say anything." Amanda nodded and took a breath. "You are so beautiful, and yet you walk around with this weight..."

Amanda's eyes bugged at the words "with this weight." Was he calling her fat? Her eyes began to well with tears.

"Listen," Morris said sharply. A co-worker entered the lounge, and Amanda ducked her head to hide her watery eyes. A racecar sped around her mind, not stopping. It was a dizzying affect, and had Morris not been holding her shoulders, she would have fallen into his chest. *Weight?* Sometimes she wished she had not grown so close to Morris at work. She used to be able to hide in plain sight and only speak when spoken to. *Do my work; don't make a sound,* she had thought. *Take home my check because what else matters.* But Morris would not allow her to continue on that path. No, he was the life of the party, and he was determined to drag Amanda, scraped knees and elbows, along the way.

> "Do not join those who drink too much wine or gorge themselves on meat, for drunkards and gluttons become poor, and drowsiness clothes them in rags." Proverbs 23:20-21(CEB)

Kai

I'm sorry I missed the signs. Well, I didn't miss the sign that something was off with you, and my life was just so full with the newness of motherhood. I'm sorry I heard in your voice the fright, the slurring, the pretend excitement when you heard the squealing of my newborn in the background. I heard the disappointment when I told you I had to go and would call you back, but didn't for weeks. I'm sorry I asked a mutual friend to check in on you because I was really worried but couldn't offer the extra time to talk and visit, so I relied on her to be me, not knowing I was your lifeline. My heart broke when you called me fussing because I hadn't checked on you or met up for lunch with you. You had three grown kids. I'm sorry I was late in the game and hit postpartum depression, and I thought you understood. Then I received a call that you had died, which crushed my heart because I couldn't make myself available to you, even though I knew you needed my ministry, but so did my newborn; I needed myself. You were buried on my birthday, which took me out inside because I could have prevented your death. I just hope you forgive me.

Kai was made to feel guilty of becoming a new mother. She was the strong friend, the overachiever, the perfect wife, the boss, but she was overwhelmed with guilt that she shouldn't have had to carry in the first place. A lot of times, we can be selfish creatures, continually pulling from the strong or expecting them to continue with old habits even when a huge change has impacted their life. Women normalize the birth of babies but ignore the risk, behavior, hormonal imbalances, age differences, career stress, and demands of motherhood. Being a mom is a blessing but can also bring strain to many, and that's okay. As women, we need to be more accepting and selfless as our friends, daughters, sisters, and nieces readjust their new norm of motherhood.

Kai had internal reasons for her actions. She remembered...

I heard the family gossip about how I had changed. I heard the hundreds of unwanted suggestions and the talk of me and my house being weird because we had different standards or values. I'm sorry that I was able to accomplish being there for everyone for the past twenty years, supporting everyone, even if I didn't agree with them, because I had respectable boundaries. I'm sorry I would rather stay home in PJs than pack a suitcase (because I'm type-A) just to meet the family for dinner, fearing it would knock us off our schedule. I'm sorry I don't want to be around the condescending attitudes. I'm sorry I don't want to comb my hair, pump my breast to prevent leakage in public, and sit uncomfortably on a hard bench, constrained in a girdle while my stitches still heal. I was crushing it in a senior-level career, but I had to learn this thing called motherhood that millions accomplished. I secretly dealt with postpartum due to adding my burden on others, or the lack of knowledge of the diagnoses among my friends and family who had never experienced it. Some of them had kids much younger, along with extra help that had been there to relieve them, and I didn't want to address the gossip of those whom had never been in my shoes.

For the family and friends who genuinely understand the newness of motherhood to a woman who wants to crush it, thank you for being patient with me and your other friends during this journey. Something new shows up every day. That energy that was put into you, and the energy I have put into accomplishing my career, I need to put into motherhood. I'm alone and dying inside, partially by choice. My husband's schedule is consumed, my depression won't allow me to be bothered, and my pride won't let me admit that I feel like a failure because I don't know why the baby is crying all night every night this week. Before going back to work, I created a great routine and weaned my baby off breastmilk, but he cried to stay up and play from 1:00 a.m. to 4:00 a.m. I didn't know the new formula was going to constipate him so badly, so the nursery called me to get him, due to his excessive crying my first week back to work. He's chilling now, watching cartoons without a cry, but I'm stressed about what work is thinking of my rapid exit.

I was embarrassed when my co-worker asked what I wasted on my blouse. Nobody told me that breastmilk may still produce under stress-triggered situations. While giving a presentation, my breasts decided to leak milk. The baby came five months ago, so when will the tears stop? Now it's a severe diaper rash from the introduction to food; I've never seen a tush so red and sore. Oh my God, what happened to the sweet-smelling poop? I just passed out from this new stench.

This was a great week, I thought to myself as I drove into work. *What's that smell?* My therapist suggested music to help control my postpartum in the course of changing roles. I have a secret love for hip hop; it gets me hyped for the work day. *Let me check my shoes...that's a horrid smell.* I was winning again; coffee was ready for me. The breasts completely dried up, and the baby was happy as I checked him on the nursery cameras. *I think I need to throw that diaper pail away; it's not working. I can smell baby poop, and the smell is embedded in my nostrils.* I started my morning huddle, and my staff mentioned they smelled poop and baby lotion or powder. Strangely, I've been smelling that all morning. My assistant whispered to me that I had baby poop on the hip of my pants. "Oh, darn, I lost again this morning."

As mothers new or continuing, we should not strive to be perfect. We are human and will make mistakes. If God blesses you with motherhood, think of it as a journey. Sometimes we have to adjust who we are in order to make it through.

"No doubt about it, children are a gift from the LORD; the fruit of the womb is a divine reward." Psalms 127:3(CEB)

Kelli

How can someone get everything they ever wanted or asked for in life? Does life work that easily? I mean, by a blink of an eye, whatever they want magically appears. It could be something as simple and normal as growing up in a wealthy two-parent home, venturing off overseas to discover themselves, or learning their identity before wasting time in the wrong major in college or professional career. They get every job they apply for, even if they are not really interested in that field of study. They are able to start their life debt free, with no prior bills in their name or student loan debt and their first car paid for. They even marry the perfect husband who is handsome, loving, attentive, supportive, wealthy, and giving—a man of God. It's just amazing how perfect one's life can be.

When asked about it, Kelli said that she prayed and had faith in God. She had continuous faith in God's will for her life. She abided by God's way and was reassured that He provided her with her every need. She never worried or stressed because she knew God would make a way. I guess Kelli learned and developed a strong faith and dedication to God early in life. It always seemed like her life was easy.

She was often envied for her perfect life, as well as her parents' choices that provided an opportunity for her to enjoy life instead of growing up fast and having to be independent. Many think that they are strong but are truly tired underneath it all. Does struggling through life, feeling exhausted from constantly jumping over hurdles, indicate that there may be a lack of faith? The overwhelming feeling of worry due to an uneasy lifestyle often makes me fear that I might be praying the wrong prayer. Is it possible that some sins are passed down from the choices and decision of our parents?

> "God the Father chose you because of what he knew beforehand. He chose you through the Holy Spirit's work of making you holy and because of the faithful obedience and sacrifice of Jesus Christ. May God's grace and peace be multiplied to you." 1 Peter 1:2(CEB)

Samantha

Have you ever been in a situation where you had to "play a role" or "put on a face" to survive a moment? Sam often had to play a role that wasn't herself to keep up appearances and facades, as well as to appease her mother.

Our family was coming over, and Sam was obligated to play hostess and pretend all was well. She needed put on a show in which every family member was welcomed, every family member was loved. There was nothing wrong with this family picture. In this family, no one raised their voice or spoke out of turn. No one brought up delicate subject matter (and none existed). Not today. Not ever. As the eldest daughter, the responsibility of always playing the role fell on Sam, and over the years, she'd mastered it. There could be no hint of unbalance, no tension felt, no table cloth askew or dish cold. Perfection was the only option.

She rolled her shoulders back so that she was not slouching. This was an unconscious correction, and it was automatic. She could hear her mother's voice ringing in her ear: "Don't slouch, child. People will think you are uncultured and uncared for." Those rebuking words would be accompanied by the pain of fingernails digging into her skin to emphasize the gravity of her slight. Those nails, freshly painted and pointed, made deep indentations, and although it had been well over ten years since Sam's mother had used that method to remind her of her shortcomings, the memory itself was enough to bring back the pain in her shoulder.

She shifted uncomfortably, quickly looking over her other shoulder. Her mother did not like to see or show pain, or emotion at all, for that matter. "You must grin and bear it," she would say. Even excitement had to be tempered to a slight smile. She told Sam that one must not be overly cheerful, as it may be off-putting to those around you. You never wanted to be one of those people.

Over the years, Sam had to remind herself that she was no longer under her mother's roof, but today, she would have to play the role of the perfect daughter. Today, she would again have to live a lie.

"Darling, your house looks so…"

Sam waited for the criticism, but she did not care what her mother thought about her home. She'd purchased it with no help from her parents, and therefore, she could do with it what she wanted. Her color scheme was loud, to choose a word from her mother's crass thinking of certain groups that made up their ethnicity. What her mother did not know was that her daughter had chosen those loud colors because she wanted her house to have a voice—a voice she had not been able to have any other time in her life. Her home would speak for her. It would tell the things that made her excited and nostalgic. It would **not** hold secrets.

Sam quickly glanced toward a bookshelf. Snuggled between three very large encyclopedias was a journal—well, several journals—and in that book were her hopes, her dreams, and the disparate parts of her life. She would write about the things her family refused to address, then publish them in magazines. She had quite a following, and she was proud of her accomplishment. The writing was therapeutic and monetarily rewarding. Her mother would be scandalized to know that her daughter was airing the family's dirty laundry for the world to smell, see, and almost touch, but it was her attempt at normalcy that led the eldest daughter to write.

The sound of a bass guitar banged out an indefinable sound, and Sam smiled. She'd had that installed three weeks ago, far before she would know that her mother would insist on the family dinner being held at her home instead of Bon Vivant, the family homestead. When Sam was seven, her mother found those French words and slapped the name on the house, and the family was to call the home by that name ever since.

> "Children, obey your parents in everything, because this pleases the Lord. Parents, don't provoke your children in a way that ends up discouraging them. Slaves, obey your masters on earth in everything. Don't just obey like people pleasers when they are watching. Instead, obey with the single motivation of fearing the Lord. Whatever you do, do it from the heart for the Lord and not for people. You know that you will receive an inheritance as a reward. You serve the Lord Christ. But evildoers will receive their reward for their evil actions. There is no discrimination." Colossians 3:20-25(CEB)

Evelynn

I tried—I really, really did—and blood is everywhere. Should I go to the hospital or sit in the shower until it all washes away? He can't find out; he will not find out. I've come too far, but I failed yet again. I counted thoroughly, marking and planning on my calendar app. I lost weight, ate healthy, and worked out. I took meds and even stood upside down in a handstand. I took my temperature and checked my pH balance and specific gravity. This is the third partner I failed. I just know he will divorce me. Leave me for a real woman. I couldn't tell him up front. Should I have told him up front, that it didn't work in my last relationship? The wedding was called off, all because I was being honest with the love of my life. Why would I put my weaknesses up front and risk an eligible bachelor the opportunity to wed me? I deserve happiness, not punishment; my one failure shouldn't make me a cat lady. I will continue to try until I succeed. He cannot find out. "Google, what time is it?" Okay, I still have time to release, clean, and sleep off the pain with a Percocet. I've learned from my prior two marriages and three boyfriends not to notify them of the good news ahead of time. Thank God it was only ten weeks. No physical evidence or inquiry from him, which means no explanation.

Oh my God, it hurts so bad. Maybe I should go to the ER; then again, the pain can't be as bad as him finding out and leaving me. I can take it. Let me spray bleach and take this Percocet. I can try again in a few weeks, and everything will be okay. Don't worry, we got this, just let me sleep. Why are these tears falling? I'll add an Ativan too.

"Google, what's Joseph's ETA?" Okay, I can sleep this off for two hours. "Google, wake me in two hours." Then I can reapply my makeup and prepare dinner. He won't know...just fall asleep already. Rest, relax, calm down. The pain has weakened, but these tears won't stop. Okay, mind, relax, it takes thirty minutes for Ativan to kick in. Did I clean all the blood up? I forgot to toss my clothes in the trash outside. Oh no, let me do that. He can't find out...no one can know. Everyone will be talking about me. Who loses nine pregnancies? My mom thinks I can't get pregnant, but I can get pregnant...I just don't stay pregnant. Yawn...

> "As you do not know the path of the wind, or how the body is formed in a mother's womb, so you cannot understand the work of God, the Maker of all things."
> Ecclesiastes 11:5(CEB)

Have you ever felt less than a woman because you could not produce? Evelynn was knocking on forty and had numerous miscarriages and product of conceptions. People are not conscious of the stress, effort, panic, and anxiety many women go through to get pregnant and stay pregnant for a full term. Men can be insensitive and not mentally prepared to accept that their wife may not be able to do something that's supposed to be natural, something we are created to do. Friends and family members may not realize that asking "simple" questions such as, "When are you going to have a baby?" or "Do you like kids?" and those witless jokes about being over thirty-five years of age and at risk, referencing a woman's eggs as old or scrambled, or mentioning a child will have a disability by waiting so long can send a woman into a manic state of hiding miscarriages. Evelynn has lost the sense of grieving; she's become numb to losing a child. Now, what should be joyful is a win-or-lose competition, an addiction, and Evelynn is unwilling to accept her truth.

"Blessed are those who mourn, for they will be comforted." Matthew 5:4(CEB)

Keisha

Through sickness and health...more like through fraud and fraud. I haven't slept with my husband in two years—post the day we said, "I do." I almost thought I should turn my life over to the nunnery. Miserable, wondering why he won't touch me anymore, looking at our relationship in a romantic way, rage and anger is all I get. We dated for a year before we married, and everything was blissful and plentiful, including the sex. Once we were married, however, it all ceased. I often wondered if it was medical. How could it just cease? Umm...could it be another woman? My friend's husband stopped having sex with her because he had another woman and was too tired to perform and keep up with her hyper-sexuality. She did *everything* sexual, and his interest was still elsewhere. I decided to try more. I stepped out of character and performed a striptease, performed oral, initiated a massage, and even served him dinner in an apron. Nothing worked. I'm under forty, but could this be life? Is this a hall pass to cheat? No matter how often I prayed to God, I still had an itch that needed fulfillment. My friend cheated, and her husband didn't notice. Do you think I would get caught? Or should I ask him if he might be okay with an open arrangement. I could ask if he wanted a threesome. Maybe we should seek help from the pastor, or perhaps a therapist. Gees, this is embarrassing.

For years, I've had issues with my back, so I tried a highly recommended chiropractor since mine moved away. He was awesome and seemed very familiar, like we had met in a past life. He was easy to talk to, and the connection was automatic—so automatic that it scared me to a level that made me uncomfortable to be around him. The more appointments I went too, the more comfortable I became, and the more our conversations became therapeutic for the both of us. His nursing staff was always pleased to see me, for I apparently made his mood better. When I was not there he would not engage in small talk, but when I had an appointment he was talkative and would reveal information about himself. The nursing staff was able to learn about their boss because of me.

Usually, his intern or associate would do my adjustment and he would only follow up, but one day, he performed my adjustment himself. That adjustment went beyond an *adjustment*…having sex in the exam room was highly unprofessional, but it happened so naturally, so passionately. I was so fulfilled. Our connection and attraction were so strong. I didn't even worry about having his staff hear us or walk in on us. At that moment, the stress of my life was released, and that release was long overdue. He got up, and we looked at each other, unable to speak of what had happened. We gathered ourselves and proceeded with the appointment like nothing had happened. As I exited the room, he went to his next patient.

At this point, my follow-ups were weekly. Each visit was a form of therapy, a release from my real-life situations. The funny part was that we were discussing my home and work life. I thought I was in love again, and now I'm trying to find out how to get out of my marriage. I could really see myself married to him—young, successful, down to earth, with an arrogance which gives that sexy, dominant feel. He knows how to talk and comfort me in need. Divorce attorney on line one, please.

Then, while discussing healthcare one day, it all fell down. He said I was lucky to have a special connection to get the best doctors and that his wife works in a hospital and couldn't get a renowned physician of her choosing. *Wait.... did he say "wife?"* In my head, I ignored everything else and was stuck on "wife." *I mean, I'm married, so why am I so stunned?* He went on to say that they had been in disagreement about her delivery plan. *What the hell...wife...and baby?* I think I missed the headline of this story. My heart sunk. I just wanted to run and cry from the confusion. I felt betrayed, cheated on, but how? *I'm married as well.* My ears shut off, and I was left in confusion. I ran to my car and cried. *Again why did I decided to cheat?* We cheated on our spouses together. It was good, and we developed a connection. *I'm pissed...he was supposed to be my next husband.* With my healthcare connections, I researched his wife and found out she's a doctor. *What the hell does he want with me? She's beautiful, successful, and carrying his unborn child. How could he do that to his wife? Why didn't he tell me about her before?* He was always a listening ear for me. Did I maximize the conversation to the point where he couldn't vent, and was I paying a copay to see him?

I went to the next follow-up as usual, and the spark was gone for me. He asked what was wrong, but I couldn't muster the words, "You have a wife and baby you never mentioned, and we've been having sex for six months." How could I fuss when I'm a wife and mother myself? I just told him I was cramping. At the next appointment, he made an attempt toward me, and I jumped off the table in fear. He was tired of my reluctance and asked if I was sleeping with my husband again. It was easier for me to lie and say yes. He then understood and said he was still not getting any from his wife, but he agreed with having only one sexual partner at a time. I'll be, now he has morals...

> "Marriage must be honored in every respect, with no cheating on the relationship, because God will judge the sexually immoral person and the person who commits adultery." Hebrews 13:4(CEB)

See, God allows us to go through certain "seasons," and He brings certain individuals into our lives, as a part of His plan. He knows our purpose and our destiny in life. We just sometimes lack faith to strictly follow His Word. We often allow life and worldly situations to take over, which is very easy to do. The stressors and intimidations of life will force us into doing things that are not a part of God's plan, but ours. Sometimes our plans can become dreadful for us because we start to engage and fall for money, success, love, or greed at a rapid pace. We can lose focus on serving God and following His Word because our way is getting us there faster. We then accept things that are poisonous for us or threatening to us, and we often develop depression because we would rather accept treatment that's not right for us just to gain those tangible items, gifts, fame, praise, wealth, or notoriety, which lead to our quick demise.

> "God has made everything fitting in its time, but has also placed eternity in their hearts, without enabling them to discover what God has done from beginning to end." Ecclesiastes 3:11 (CEB)

Oftentimes, we avoid those who try to push the Word on us. We even turn our back on those who reference the Word when we just want to vent. Therefore, a distance is created because we may not be on that spiritual level to accept guidance or encouragement from that person because of the faith they may possess. You know what? It's okay. Everyone comes around in their own timing, which is why God gives us grace and mercy. He knew we would struggle with life and worldly possessions—it happened in his time. The key is finding your way back to those believers to help reassure you of His Word, as well as getting back on track before it's too late.

Simone

"I am calling her now. She deserves to know the truth about her lying donkey of a husband."

"How could he? Who does he think he is?"

"This was two years of my life he was playing with, and I am not having that. I'm not being the fool!"

Have you ever been in a situation where you thought you were number one in someone's life, the love of their life, the apple of their eye, when it turned out you were actually the other woman? Well, meet Simone—the other woman.

The other night, he left his phone unlocked on the bed while using the bathroom. I scrolled through it clandestinely, making sure he was still busy in the bathroom. I was looking for one number in particular—his wife's. Yes, and don't judge me too harshly. I am not a homewrecker or something like that, but his wife had the right to know that he was cheating on her. My best friend, Pam, told me the other day that I was wrong for getting involved with him in the first place, but I don't see it that way. This man was meant for me. It was not my fault that he was tied to a wife who was no good. If he loved her, he would not be coming over here so much. If she was giving him all he needed, he wouldn't need me.

What changed, you might ask? What would make me, after two years of loving him in secret, finally tell his wife? During that same clandestine perusal through his phone, I stumbled upon three other women he had been talking to. While I was in love, excusing the fact that he had a wife because I just knew I was his true love, this dude here was running through women in the city.

That night, I sat down on the bed, stunned. I no longer cared if he caught me with his phone. I didn't care about being sneaky anymore.

I just wanted to know: *what other woman had he been sleeping with?!*

At first, the plan was to tell his wife to let him go. She was the reason we could not be together; the reason he could not be with me every night. I had planned to send her a short, hot video of his head between my legs, giving me great satisfaction. I had hoped to get her so upset that she would put him out of the house and he would have no choice but to come to me. Now, I just planned to inform her of his infidelities and hoped that she took him for all he had—which couldn't be much because I was practically paying for all of our outings.

I sat on my bed cross-legged, then took a deep breath. I tried not to think of all the bad that could come out of this conversation.

What if she doesn't answer?

What if she hangs up before I finish explaining who I am?

What if she...?

There were many what-ifs, but I was set on coming clean. He needed to be punished for his part in my heartache. I put the television on mute. I was watching reruns of *Scandal* as I dialed her number, positioning myself on the bed and digging in for what would be a difficult situation—for her, because I was all cried out.

The phone rang, and on the fifth ring, a warm voice answered with a husky "Hello?"

"Umm, yes, hi, is this Kenneth's wife?"

A low chuckle followed my question. "Whose calling?" she asked with a smile in her voice.

Immediately, I felt that she was laughing at me.

"This is his girlfriend, Simone."

"Well, Simone, it is good to finally hear from you. I cannot say I am surprised by this call."

I paused at this. *What does she mean by that? Did Kenneth tell her about our blow-up? I mean, I did hit him in the face a few times, but that was warranted.* I was pissed.

"Excuse me?"

"No need to be excused dear. We are having a conversation, yes?"

I cleared my throat. "You...knew I would be calling?"

"Well, when my husband showed up at three o'clock in the morning with welts on his face and neck, I knew it had to be a woman."

She waited a beat then asked, "So, what did he do?"

"I found out he was cheating on me," I answered indignantly.

Another chuckle from her end. "Oh, yea?"

"Yes, and I thought you needed to know about his ole trifling-tail ways."

"So, let me ask you a question...Simone, was it?"

"Yes, it's Simone."

"How long have you been with Kenneth? Seeing him, I mean," she clarified for me.

"Humph," I hummed into the phone. "Two years," I answered her question, feeling a gut punch again.

"So, all this time, you were okay to lay with him and stay with him, knowing he had a wife at home? Why not call me in the first month, the second, or the third? Why now?"

I was caught off guard by her questions. I had no comeback other than the truth: "I just thought you should know."

"Hmm. Let me ask you, Simone, how often does Kenneth take you out? You know, to dinner, a movie, stuff like that?"

"He doesn't usually. He says you spend all his money. He has bought me groceries occasionally though."

"Hmm, do you want to know why he has only bought you groceries?"

"Because you spend the money," I say hotly.

"No, Simone, because that is his weekly allowance," she chuckled heavily.

I felt my face heat, realizing I had made a mistake with this call.

"See, Kenneth brings his check home to me. And yes, he makes good money. Our bills are payed on time, and my home is beautifully laid. I want for nothing at all because his money comes home. He has to give you something, and this he knows, so what do you get? A few bags of groceries, and he gets a cheap thrill or ride, whatever your specialty is. You realize you have been giving up prime or used goods for groceries… for two years? That's not enough, honey."

I was shocked into silence. She was still speaking, but I remained quiet on my end. My face once again heated, and I felt steam rise from my ears. I quickly scrolled through my phone for the short video and sent it to her number, while she continued to tell me all the ways her husband had mistreated me.

There was a pause in her spiel, and I held my breath, waiting for her hysteria on the other end. It did not come, but was did roll out sent a chill down my spine. She no longer chuckled, but she now full-out belly laughed. She laughed so hard that tears began to pool in my eyes. At that moment, I was so glad I decided not to do this face to face. *I am a fool!*

"Girl," she said between pants of laughter. *"You. Have. Been. Cheated."* She emphasized each word.

I should hang up, I know it. Why am I subjecting myself to this conversation? But a part of me wanted to hear what she had to say, as if this was my punishment for dealing with this for two years.

"What do you mean?" I practically sobbed into the phone, my anger giving way to overwhelming defeat.

"Baby girl, I hate to tell you, but when Kenneth gave me my oral transactions, I could barely see the top of his forehead. Most nights I only saw his hair sticking from between my legs."

My stomach rolled as she described sex with her husband—my boyfriend. It was graphic and very detailed. In the end, she thanked me for putting in so much work so she did not have to.

"Doll," she said to me as we ended the conversation, "you are not the first, and surely you will not be the last he cheats with. I am just biding my time until my baby becomes of age. Cause guess what? Then and only then will I let him go. Until the time *I* see fit, he will continue to take care of the home. Be sure of this: I will *never* settle for some *groceries* if I'm giving out *goods,* because mine do not come cheap. Yours should not either. Goodbye!"

By the time she hung up, I was lying on my bed, feeling small and so unsure. A call I had been waiting so long to make turned me every which way but loose. *Now what*? Why did I believe he would leave his wife for me? How did I get so wrapped up in him that I devalued myself? How did a life of marriage and kids flash before my eyes? How and when did I become so gullible, so naïve, such a *fool*!

> "He who commits adultery is senseless. Doing so, he destroys himself. He is wounded and disgraced. His shame will never be wiped away." Proverbs 6:32-33 (CEB)

Girl, it's time for self-reflection!

Do you know anyone who is like any of these women?

Have you ever judged a woman in one of these situations?

Did you see *yourself* in any of these women? Wait now…**Be honest.**

Do you know how to get your Lyfe?

Are you ready for a second go at life, due to missed opportunities, divorce, or trauma?

Do you believe in forgiveness?

What about new beginnings?

Girl, just continue on…let's get your Lyfe!

Girl, What's Your Battle?

Do you know most women—or should I say, most people—are unaware of their feelings? They don't know the sources of their feelings or the reasons behind certain decisions they make. They just know that life is hard, and they are trying to deal with it. Sometimes in life, we feel a sense of anxiousness, and we might even have anxiety or panic attacks that render our progression in life static. We gain or lose an excessive amount of weight without a known cause. We would rather Netflix alone than socialize with others. Without noticing, we sometimes go from being erratic to sweet and loving within twenty minutes. We feel our skin crawling or itching one second then we become sleepy the next. Thoughts of suicide or self-harm might set in as a way to cope. We begin to feel a certain mental or physical impairment that may be holding us back, so it is imperative that we place everything on pause and do a self-check.

Start your self-check by taking a day off from life. Nothing is wrong with taking a mental day off from work or school to recharge. Journal when the anxious feelings occur. Try to recognize your triggers right when they occur by writing your exact feelings at that moment. Don't worry about your writing being legible or if you are rambling. Once you are in a better state, you can later evaluate your feelings or the exact trigger. If certain situations cause anxiety, panic, or a mental breakdown more than three times in your lifetime, you need to immediately remove that situation from your life. People, or even a single person such as a loved one, can also give you anxious and panicky feelings, so make sure that same rule applies to people in your life. Listen to your body's internal alert system, especially with others. Remove them, leave them, and separate all dealings with them.

As young girls, we are taught how to cope with certain situations. When faced with an uncomfortable feeling, we often ignore our body's defense system just so that things do not become so complicated. We are sometimes very quiet and complacent; we say that we are tired, but we are not really physically tired. At times, we can forcefully hold a smile, but then it disappears, and we find ourselves in a daze, looking into thin air, at nothing specifically. Often we want to be left alone, isolated so that we don't have to pretend any more. We cancel plans we have made because it's hard to mustard up the courage to be around other individuals. Some people even get lost in a musical world or a mystical world of literature to pass time. That offers some relief, as we do not immediately deal with the current issue at hand. Learning to cope with certain situations sends a signal to our body that forces it to relax and accept something or somebody that can put a stop, delay, or drought in a simple life plan. Perhaps they are causing mental illness, physical harm, body complexes, or self-esteem issues. Maybe they are creating addictions that lead to a person being perceived as lazy, when they are really depressed but coping. Whether overweight or underweight, they may be utilizing food as a tool to cope. They might become an alcoholic, a pill popper, or a meth head, using drugs as a form of coping to help ease the anxious feeling. Coping techniques present themselves in many forms, and society has encouraged women and young girls to ignore the body's warning to make one feel better about themselves.

Girl, how do your respond to stress?

The way you respond to a situation or react to stress is not always the way of life. Your instant response is not the final outcome. You will sometimes have to change the way you respond, the way you react, and adjust your perspective and attitude of the situation, if you realize your attitude is always negative, abusive, or draining to your soul. By changing your reactions, you can actually set the tone of certain situations and totally reduce some, if not all, of the stress and anxiety in most situations.

I know you are probably saying, "It's easier said than done," but try it! Practice doing it. Change the way you react for twenty-eight days, and see if it helps.

In some cases, you may have to take off that mask or that superhero cape. You may need to take a step away from everything and check yourself into a wellness center or therapy, or maybe seek advice from a life coach. In life, we cannot always help ourselves with an issue, even if we have prayed about it, read about it, and walked away from it, especially if some issues are more deeply rooted. Nothing is wrong with seeking additional help.

This anxious girl or depressed girl might have been holding things down for her entire family for years, hiding abuse for years, keeping secrets for everyone for a lifetime. Perhaps she has been the savior to everyone she encountered—the role model, the one with the answers, the teacher, the preacher, the emphatic one. Most people who experience that level of anxiousness are selfless. She will not vent to anyone, due to feeling like she's pushing her heavy weight upon them. She will find ways to cope to keep up the appearance that she is fine and happy, but she will continue to suffer in silence.

We must remember that it is always important for us to get ourselves together, and we must be our own priority. It's okay to give and help others, but when our vessel is empty, when do we find time to refuel? You must address your issues from their roots before you end up lifeless. Remember, a man may not be available at all times to support you during a major time of need or in the exact moment of your breakdown or demise. With the help of both a medical professional and God, girl, you can get your life. It's okay if you are diagnosed with anxiety, depression, ADD/ADHD, bipolar disorder, schizophrenia, or post-traumatic stress disorder, as long as you take time to tend to yourself and take proper action.

Remember, God is unlike man. He will not hold certain battles, mistakes, grudges, habits, or the past against us. Like an old hymn says, He grants us new mercies every morning. God knows what we will do before we even do it, and He allows us to battle some things to strengthen us for something else. Even if you have veered from His plan or purpose for your life. He will not change your calling. He knew that you would fail or fall for a weakness; He is not surprised at anything that you might get yourself into. However, He expects us to learn, develop, and grow from our mistakes, decisions, and problems. If God has promised it, you will get it. He can put you in a position that will restore everything you have lost, and He can provide new beginnings each day. You must trust and have faith in Him, realize your issues, and be willing to put in the necessary work.

Closed Doors

Do you know that God will close some doors because He knows you are worth so much more than that relationship, job, house, or car? You may have wanted that thing or person, or perhaps you thought and prayed for that career or house, but God saw greater down the road and closed that door. He knew you didn't need that extra stress or the trouble that was going to be brought on by it. Trouble was awaiting you, and guess what? God helped you dodge it. It is imperative that you change your outlook on certain situations. Not everything is bad. Being positive, really having faith, and understanding God's mercy can help you through depression and anxiety.

> "I will say to God, my solid rock, 'Why have you forgotten me? Why do I have to walk around, sad, oppressed by enemies?' With my bones crushed, my foes make fun of me, constantly questioning me: 'Where's your God now?' Why, I ask myself, are you so depressed? Why are you so upset inside? Hope in God! Because I will again give him thanks, my saving presence and my God."
> Psalms 42:9-11 (CEB)

Girl, Know Yourself

You can't expect someone to know your true identity if you don't know and accept yourself and your faults. Learn yourself and be open to the truth about yourself. Know your behavior and your traits. Are you an empath, a narcissist, or an egotist? Don't worry, there is no wrong answer.

Empaths have a caring nature about everyone, including strangers. They will attract and be attracted to a unique curiousness, outside of normal circumstances. They are great listeners and offer vulnerability to make others comfortable. Rather than focusing on themselves, empaths naturally find others or put more attentions into others. Empaths are never satisfied with basic answers; instead, they must know the ins and outs of everything. They will never criticize your way of life, and they will even put themselves in your situation before assisting you or offering a solution, even if unwanted. Empaths are very ambitious, and they love to see progression and are the best supporters. They will be alongside you, both physically and mentally. They don't focus on any negativity but seek satisfaction in overcoming one's obstacles. Although this often drains them, most empaths don't have a cut-off limit, and they can easily be taken advantage of.

Narcissist are completely in love with themselves. Beyond the notion of having just high self-esteem, they need constant praise, which may come from a certain sense of entitlement. They often lack empathy and always exaggerate about their accolades, physique, and talents. It's rare for narcissists to notice what's going around them in the physical or the people they engage with daily. Narcissist can sometimes live in a fantasy world that highlights them being the best, having the best, being the star player, or having the highest status of all of their friends and family members. The downside of narcissism is that this fantasy world is their way of controlling feelings of insignificance, loneliness, emptiness, or loss of control of their life. To keep that adrenaline super high, they will belittle others and point out their flaws to hide their own shortcomings. A narcissist cannot help it and will take advantage of others, all because they can secretly envy others. They know how to manipulate things to work in their favor, including physical items and arguments.

Egoists only take into consideration and are often only motivated by things of their own self-interest. It's hard to find people to satisfy their ego, so finding and staying in a relationship is difficult for egoists. They are very aggressive and revengeful, and they can degrade people by saying that someone's way of thinking or acting is stupid. Sometimes egoists enjoy bragging about how their way is better than others. They can find or create enemies out of nowhere, and they often prefer to pose alone in pictures. Most of what they do is based on how something can benefit them. Dealing with an egoist can be really tough and even dangerous. It is important to know how to identify an egoist so that you can decide to avoid or learn how to accept them. It's hard for an egoist to fall in love with others, and if you fall in love with an egoist you might have to convince them that you are a big catch. Perhaps learn methods of talking them into believing that you are the best thing ever. Identifying yourself as an egoist may explain why your partner, family, or friends feel isolated from you.

> "I say be guided by the Spirit and you won't carry out your selfish desires. A person's selfish desires are set against the Spirit, and the Spirit is set against one's

selfish desires. They are opposed to each other, so you shouldn't do whatever you want to do. But if you are being led by the Spirit, you aren't under the Law. The actions that are produced by selfish motives are obvious, since they include sexual immorality, moral corruption, doing whatever feels good, idolatry, drug use and casting spells, hate, fighting, and obsession, losing your temper, competitive opposition, conflict, selfishness, group rivalry, jealousy, drunkenness, partying, and other things like that. I warn you as I have already warned you, that those who do these kinds of things won't inherit God's kingdom. But the fruit of the Spirit is love, joy, peace, patience, kindness, goodness, faithfulness, gentleness, and self-control. There is no law against things like this. Those who belong to Christ Jesus have crucified the self with its passions and its desires. If we live by the Spirit, let's follow the Spirit. Let's not become arrogant, make each other angry, or be jealous of each other." Galatians 5:16-26(CEB)

Girl, Don't Drown!

Are you being the anchor for others? Do you feel yourself drowning yet? Sometimes you can be the anchor for family, friends, co-workers, or your mate, but you could be drowning because no one seems to notice because they only see you as strong. You may feel tired, angered, stressed, disgruntled, or negative, without knowing why.

Girl, let go…or pull that anchor up!

There is no reason for you to be the one having to hold it down for everyone. You are fading away, the air is being sucked out of you, your soul has levitated, and you are lying flat on the floor, lifeless. Who will even notice you once you are gone, physically there but mentally elsewhere? Who has stopped to ask themselves to check on your mental health before they unloaded their burdens onto you? Do you have someone to confide in?

If you are the one who constantly dumps on a friend, family member, or partner, stop and think about that person's well-being before you anchor them with your load. Boundaries should be set to ensure that someone is able to tolerate their own issues. Some people put themselves in the same situation, time after time, without ever learning from their mistakes or mishaps, then they expect a listening ear or someone to be there, not realizing that they are constantly lowering a person's anchor and contributing to mental exhaustion or a breakdown.

Are You a Good Friend?

Sometimes it's great to sit back and make sure we are not contributing to someone else's anchor. Are you really a good girlfriend? Do you establish relationships without motives and add value to your friendships? It is important that you don't constantly drain others or put a damper on them when you are in their presence. Is it easy for you to pick up where you left off with a friend, without holding on to resentment or resistance, even if you've been distant for some time, or is life just so full that time hasn't permitted you to do so? When you have been hurt by a friend, are you quick to throw stones? Do you realize that everyone lives in a glass house and you can potentially hurt that friend and contribute to their downward spiral for being a tad bit selfish? After all, if you are true friends, you both should be able to express your feelings in a respectful manner.

A good friend should be empowering, prayerful, and not afraid to fill a void, but at the same time, they should not always expect to fill every void in your life. Part of being a good friend is being seen as a priority, being able to accept, understand, and help your friend work through some faults they may be experiencing, without judgment, especially if you decide to stay in their life.

Girl, Are You Insecure?

Do you suffer from insecurities in life? Do you hide behind false confidence and being extra or loud all the time because you are really insecure? Have you heard that value plus vulnerability, minus the trust of others, can create insecurities?

You can place value on something or someone so much that you begin to start feeling vulnerable. Then, it is easy for you to end up not really trusting that person or thing. Often, you can feel that something won't work out, it's not going to be okay, or that person won't come through. Then this overwhelming feeling of fear sets in, and you are concerned that something might happen if you trust that person. At that point, you are creating unnecessary levels of insecurities.

Do you create these hallucinatory situations in your head to make yourself feel that everything is great? You tell yourself that you are perfect in every way, you are the stuff when in reality, you are not and everything is *not* okay! You ignore the red flags and trust everything because you are so insecure and you feel that's all you deserve. You might even constantly surround yourself with friends who are doing less than you, or dealing with addictions, or are in abusive situations, just to feel that you are succeeding in life. You've settled and have faked having high self-esteem for so long that you don't even notice when you are falling into a deep trap that can be so hard to get out of. Even if you make it out of that situation, you might end up right back in it because of your false level of security.

Wife and Motherhood

Girl, do you want to be a wife and mother? For real, think about it… Not just because the church, your mother, or society has pushed and added the pressure of being a wife and mother due to what society deems the norm for a woman's role because of the make-up of her body; they tell you a woman is supposed to be a wife and mother one day. People can even make you feel ashamed to truly admit that being a wife or mother is not your desire. Being a wife and mother holds a huge responsibility and is a job for life, which you have to be committed to 100 percent of the time; even then, you will feel like you are failing. You must be physically and mentally prepared for these roles because not only your family but society will hold you to every decision you make. A lot of times, we listen to men or the older generation to help make this decision for us, and we never truly think thoroughly about it ourselves. Girl, you have a choice. Know yourself and decide if being a wife and mother is something you want.

Remember, when we were little girls, all those fairy tales and dreams had us wishing upon a star looking for our prince. Now, as we listen to those stories as a woman, wife, daughter, mother, or boss, we feel like that little girl who lost her dreams, forgot about her dreams, or deferred her dreams because she no longer saw that magic. Real life hit her, and she didn't know the true meaning of following her dreams, the initial start behind wishing upon that star. Her worth and struggles truly had nothing to do with retrieving the prince; the prince was looked at as prize. He picked her out of everyone, when really, her focus should have been about looking inside herself, gaining determination and strength, learning her worth, and believing in miracles to accomplish her dream. Actually, that prince was just a bonus for her believing in herself or some form of accomplishment.

When it comes to marriage, I think the wedding wins over more women than actually being the wife. At your wedding, you get to be a princess for the day…you have your prince charming at the end of the aisle, you dance, you feast, you feel the love in the air, until you wake up from the fairy tale and real marital situations hit you dead in your gut! Your husband cheats, he slaps you in your face, your house is in foreclosure…vacant soul! A stranger is in your house…you ask yourself, "Who is this person?"

Becoming one as husband and wife is not always easy, and that's okay. Marriage is not that fairy tale we once dreamed of. Once awakened, your personalities might clash; money problems sometimes erupt; family members can intrude; physical appearances may change; careers, dreams, or goals may be placed on hold. In marriage, compromises will need to take place. I'm sorry, but everybody can't always win at the same time, during the same season or phase of life.

It has been known that during marriage, women's lives change the most. Data shows that women are usually the unhappy one in a marriage. Why is this so, when society has helped us dream up this perfect new world that appears once we are married.

If you want to be a wife, you must know that you need to be prepared to be a wife and for the changes that come with being a wife and mother. Asking yourself if you want to be a wife and mother is a healthy question that we often ignore. It is important to think about taking on this role because it will affect your body, career, and mental health the most.

According to Paul, the main idea for marriage is companionship, to engage in sexual acts, and to reproduce, but with one chosen partner until death. After your spouse's death, you can remain single or choose to remarry. It was understood that differences may take place, but divorce is not an option. If separation took place, the woman was to remain by herself until a reconciliation with her husband.

See...this is a serious question. Do you want to be a wife?

You are not supposed to run away when things don't work out. Are you prepared for life?

Paul gave us a forewarning that marriage may not be easy. Also, Paul spoke of staying in a situation to which God has called you. Many enter a marriage before consulting with God to see if He has called them to be with that person.

You know, we sometimes ignore those red flags because we have a dream wedding in mind. The sex may be good, and you know the Good Book said sex is for married folks!

After marriage, things that took place prior to being called into a Godly situation are obsolete. Being on one accord is very important before reproducing, for if you are at odds, this poses issues onto the children. Prior to motherhood, you should be unified with your husband. However, we know it can sometimes be hard, but with proper effort and having faith to follow God's way, the work you put in should hold value in your marriage. Although divorce is not recommended, it is biblically noted that some walk away from marriage.

However, a marriage can be happy and long lasting if two evenly yoked, compatible individuals, who are called by God, are placed together for the Covenant of Marriage before God. If the two are unified and agreed upon, procreation should take place.

"If a woman has a husband who doesn't believe and he agrees to live with her, then she shouldn't divorce him. The husband who doesn't believe belongs to God because of his wife, and the wife who doesn't believe belongs to God because of her husband. Otherwise, your children would be contaminated by the world, but now they are spiritually set apart. But if a spouse who doesn't believe chooses to leave, then let them leave. The brother or sister isn't tied down in these circumstances. God has called you to peace." 1Corinthians

When making the decision of marriage, love is very important. Being in love, having love and compassion for one another, and valuing and respecting each other are vital parts of being married. Forgiving any past behaviors and lifestyles is also a must. Yes, including prostitution, pimping, or drug abuse. You must make sure you are his priority and he is yours, for this is a good start when deciding if you are ready to marry. It's important that the roles of wife and mother are well established, for many have different views of what a wife or mother should be.

Some women dream of becoming a homemaker. This kind of wife is very domestic. She's an excellent baker, number one cheerleader, and supporter. She does not mind being a server to her husband's needs, yet she can also be the sexy fox or dominatrix when the time comes. This wife has always longed to hear a house full of laughter, with little feet running through the house—a party of five. She takes pride in being the nurture, wiping away every tear, patching every wound. She desires to be the confidant, referee, and soccer mom, while living solely for her family.

Some wives want an equal partner. This type of wife is willing to support her husband's career but also has one of her own. She may want kids—perhaps two will do—but she needs help splitting the schedule with her husband. She may love to cook but doesn't have the time, yet she is great at picking up takeout. She learned domestic skills and values, but she doesn't have time to keep up with laundry and dishes every day. Therefore, the house is now in disarray.

Expectations of the roles of wife and mother should be discussed prior to marriage. Both parties need to know up front what they are willing to accept, and compromise. Many people look down on a woman who chooses a career over the home because the home is supposed to be her place, but having a spouse who understands you is all that matters. If your future husband only expects a homemaker, then follow Paul and remain single.

People like to say, "You can have it *all*!" Sadly, even at a cost, you can only juggle everything effectively for a short time before balls begin to drop, internally physically, mentally, and outwardly.

> "The Lord isn't slow to keep his promise, as some think of slowness, but he is patient toward you, not wanting anyone to perish but all to change their hearts and lives."
> 2 Peter 3:9 (CEB)

Teach Me How to Love

Girl, how do you like to be loved? It is important that you know what turns you on, what makes you feel warm and fuzzy, and that you are able to communicate your love languages. Relationships have been proven to last if each person is aware of the other's Love Language. Research has determined that there are Five Love Languages (Chapman 1995), and if a person does things that excites your love language, you will feel more appreciated in the relationship. You should also learn the Love Language of your partner or your person of interest, then decide if it is something you can incorporate into your relationship. Knowing your love language and communicating it to a person can also help that person if they are unaware. Often, someone can be doing their best to show you love, yet you can seem unmoved by it if it's not your primary love language.

Do you love receiving gifts? Perhaps you get excited, a feeling of importance or self-worth from gifts. You get a surge of excitement regardless of the size or nature of the gift. A person can give you all the time in the world or give you plenty of compliments, but if you do not receive a physical gift or a tangible item from someone, they do not reassure you of your importance to them. If this sounds familiar, Receiving Gifts may be your Love Language.

Do you need quality time from a person or a partner? Are you easily upset or sad, or do you start feeling abandoned if you don't receive a significant amount of quality time from a person? When time and focus are spent solely on you, does it warm your soul, boost your esteem, make you feel important, like you are number one in that person's life? If so, Quality Time may be your Love Language.

Do you like words of affirmation, extreme compliments, declarations of love for you? Do you thrive on praises that make you feel important, loved, or confident and secure of a person or partner in your life? Does a lack of reassuring words bother you or make you feel uncomfortable, to the point where you are not sure of one's affection or love toward you? If so, Words of Affirmation may be your Love Language.

Do you like when people do things for you, such as getting gas or an oil change for your vehicle, washing your dishes, or picking up or cooking dinner for you? Do you feel upset, angry, and unimportant to a person if they fail to do any of those things, even if they verbally express their feelings to you or buy you expensive gifts? If so, Acts of Service/Devotion may be your Love Language.

Do you like, love, or require a person or your partner to physically touch you in order to feel loved or wanted? Are you easily excited when someone cuddles or strokes your arm or leg? Do hugs validate a person's feeling toward you? Does the lack of receiving hugs, cuddles, or strokes of the arms or legs make you feel insecure, at a loss, or that you are some type of disadvantage in a person's life? If so, Physical Touch may be your Love Language.

Space is a newly added Love Language. Individuals sometimes need space in a relationship. Do you need your own space at times? Are you able to function alone, or will being alone give you a feeling of isolation? If your partner needs space, but you constantly like to do things together, or if you like to be underneath your partner at all times, this can create a problem. If both you and your partner don't have an established understanding of having space or boundaries in a relationship, jealousy can even set in. Sometimes, if a partner feels isolated or alone, they will begin to find comfort in others. If you are the one who needs the space, and your partner does not offer that space, it can lead to blowouts, resentment, or even volatile behavior patterns in the relationship.

Again…where or who taught you how to love? Where did you learn love from?

Have you ever thought about if the place you first saw love or the person who first taught you love was healthy or not? Did the love from that person present itself as a real or fake? Did that person pacify their problems in front of you? Was that love dreamable, magical, like from a fairytale romance novel, and now your expectations of love are too high? Was it traumatic? Maybe you didn't realize it was traumatic because it became your new normal, and you existed in an abusive household, which can range from molestation or physical abuse of parents or siblings to a cross up of parental roles or involvement of the parental presence in the household. Was your household abusive? Some people look at verbal and physical abuse as a way to love, and some even look at that aggressive behavior as a love language. Living in a household that's unevenly yoked can bring on unimaginable turmoil. As children, we cannot handpick the situations in which we are brought up. We do not choose our environment as kids; we do not choose our families; and we do not choose how our parents live, act, and make decisions. We must grow up and find our own way, create our own traditions, learn how to love from our standard of love and what we want, and create love. Most importantly, we must always make sure we love God first.

Finding the Blessing in the Breakup

A breakup is always hard on an individual, whether you decided to depart or the person left you. A person goes into a relationship with the intention to retain something. It can be for love, companionship, or the opportunity to complete the "American Dream," or a person can enter a relationship with the motive to benefit financially, fulfill a sexual void, or improve their physical appearance for social or career endeavors. If a relationship is brought together by God, it will rarely fail. Most are desperate for relationships, due to timelines and expectations that are put upon us. We usually have an inkling when something is not right, but we find ways to buy into the dream and ignore reality and its signs. We can have red flags flying high in front of us, but we will often pick the one thing that a person offers to make the relationship seem right.

> Girl, do you even know if you are a priority or just an option?
> Is your man willing to *make* time for you?
> Regardless of a busy work schedule or family obligations, does he still fit you in?
> If so, then you are a priority!
> Now, if he *had* time for you...

If he says, "I can see if I can fit you into my busy schedule," "I will try to fit you into my life," "My world is so consuming," "I might have spare time this weekend..."

Honey...you are an option!

Most times, we enter relationships too fast without knowing if that person is capable and willing to provide for us and meet our needs. We often skip over learning their character traits, knowing their love language, or understanding their childhood or past, which may explain how and why they choose to run a household with too many restrictions or so loosely. Some get into marriages and can't get out or divorce for fear of failure, judgement, or sin. Often, abusive, controlling, or one-sided relationships are some of the hardest to walk away from. However, it may be super easy for your partner to walk away and leave you a distressed mess. That initial sense of failure, self-doubt, lack of understanding, or loss of self-esteem can hit hard. But understanding, realizing, and accepting the blessing in the breakup will see you through it. Time invested is not a reason to stay in a relationship that God did not select for you. We often let our personal decisions speak for God, then we wonder why a relationship is not working out or why we are so miserable and hating ourselves, our partner, or our lifestyle. We could have every tangible item and still be unhappy; we could have local or national notoriety and still be unhappy. The key is to understand that your plan might not be God's plan.

> "Answer me, LORD—and quickly! My breath is fading. Don't hide your face from me or I'll be like those going down to the pit! Tell me all about your faithful love come morning time, because I trust you. Show me the way I should go, because I offer my life up to you. Deliver me from my enemies, LORD! I seek protection from you. Teach me to do what pleases you, because you are my God. Guide me by your good spirit into good

land. Make me live again, LORD, for your name's sake. Bring me out of distress because of your righteousness. Wipe out my enemies because of your faithful love. Destroy everyone who attacks me, because I am your servant." Psalms 143:7-12 (CEB)

When in or entering a relationship, it is imperative that you are able to distinguish the difference between healthy and unhealthy behavior traits. We often become so consumed in a relationship that we ignore red flags before investing time to understand them. Often, once time is invested, we feel obligated to fix a relationship or make it work. Sometimes a relationship is a waste of time because it was never meant to be, but society will condemn you or time invested will make you make the relationship work. Signs of a healthy relationship may include being able to compromise, being honest, showing mutual respect, having good communication, keeping individuality, having trust in one another, fair fighting, problem solving, having good and active sex, having self-confidence, and having control over anger. Signs of an unhealthy relationship may include being disrespected in any form, or being with someone who needs to be in constant control, who is dishonest, even if it's a small lie, who shows constant hostility, who is very dependent on you, who shows acts of intimidation, or who demonstrates sexual as well as physical violence.

Many wonder if you can turn a bad relationship good again. We all go through periods of life when stress and temptations take over our relationships. If you feel a relationship is worth saving or rekindling, you must take a few steps and put in a little work. You must figure out and re-evaluate the reason you initially got together or fell in love. Sit together and communicate the issues at hand, but be sure to hear each other out, uninterrupted. Do something special together to ensure you still enjoy each other's company, like sharing similar interests. Stop external influences from being involved, making comments, or having a say in your relationship. Come clean and be honest about things that happened or took place that caused the separation. Now, forgive each other from everything you have discussed and identified, including the hurt. Create and set boundaries that are within each other's comfort zones. In order for relationships to work, an acceptable amount of time is required between the couple. The relationship must be a priority; therefore, all other factors, including the kids or parents, must come second to the relationship.

Some relationships hit a downward spiral when the man does not feel like the provider. A provider is one of the happiest behavior types in a relationship. The provider is extremely compassionate and fully enjoys helping others. The primary goal of the provider is to make others happy. They also get a special sense of fulfillment.

At some point, you will have to learn how to let go of someone who does not really love you or is not meant for you. That is one of the hardest things to do.

> "Be strong! Be fearless! Don't be afraid and don't be scared by your enemies, because the LORD your God is the one who marches with you. He won't let you down, and he won't abandon you." Deuteronomy 31:6 (CEB)

A Guide to Overcome a Separation

Phase One – Spiritual Healing

You and your partner didn't fall in love overnight. When the realization of a loss hits, it can be tumultuous to the healing process. During the first week of your separation, give yourself time to grieve and spiritually heal.

Create a playlist – Music is a form of therapy. Sing loud, kick, scream, and yell all the things you wish you could have said but couldn't find the words yourself. Rely on that playlist to express yourself.

Pity Party – Go ahead and grant yourself a pity party for one week. Cry, eat, drink, and don't bother to put clothes on or talk to anyone. It's okay to cry, but in doing so, reflect on the situation and gain knowledge from it. Admit your wrongdoing along with his.

Turn to Faith – First, give thanks to God for His forgiveness. God knows everything and has already forgiven you for this separation. Walk through your house in prayer and cleanse your house of any negative or ill feelings. Simply talk to God as if He was your best friend. In order to move on, you need to restore your relationship with Him. Spiritual healing is needed before you can work on the outside.

Bath Time – Take a bath to feel replenished and renewed. After heavy prayer and a true conversation with God, it's time to begin the healing process for yourself. The pity party is now over. You are a survivor, and you will survive this minor setback.

The healing process takes time, but you must not fall into a slump too long. Allow yourself to release those negative feelings, then move on. It is imperative that you release those true feelings during each step of your healing. Remember, no one is judging you.

Phase Two – Survivor Mode

Create a New Playlist – Make a playlist filled with inspirational, upbeat tunes of female empowerment. No more crying, no more "I wish I should have/could have." Embrace the music, even if it's out of character for you. Remember, music is a form of therapy. Be goofy, silly, and crazy for a change. Slowly get rid of the comfort food and booze as you begin to rejoice in your own independence.

Put on Your Big Girl Panties – Admit you worshipped your husband instead of submitting to him. God does not like when we put others before Him. Yes, you followed every directive of your husband and disregarded the things that made you happy. Have a seat and apologize to those who you have shunned to please your husband. Write down changes and improvements you want to make to your house (change the curtains, paint, and rearrange the closet). Start those projects today. In your home, keep a family picture up. It is important for your kids to see the love you once had as a family.

Focus on Reviving Your Spirit – Each day, walk for thirty minutes outside, breathe the air, enjoy the view, and take in some sun. Drink plenty of water, and even try a detox if that's your thing.

Clean House – Declutter your house. Pack up all that you no longer need in a box and schedule a pick up from your local shelter or your favorite charity.

Add Some Fun to Your Life – Call a friend or family member to go out with, and just spend some time talking and laughing with them. Do something spontaneous, something out of your norm that you were restricted from doing in your marriage.

During this process, it is important to be open. In a relationship, you often learn to conform to your partner's ways or likings. Being involved with someone for a long period of time can cause you to lose your self-identity and fail to grow from a young lady into a woman.

PHASE THREE – FINDING YOUR TRUE IDENTITY

Music Therapy – You know longer have a restricted playlist. At this point in the process, you've cried, male bashed, survived, and are now in a better place. Music is still a part of your healing process. Play inspirational tunes, jazz, or easy listening stations throughout your house to set a calming, relaxing atmosphere. Perhaps even listen to these tunes during your thirty-minute walk.

Focus on Your Body – Get up, go outside, go for a walk, and enjoy Mother Nature. Start over fresh with your new healthy living choices (diet, weight-loss goal, etc.). Even dress up two days this week, wearing colors that you do not normally wear, and put on full makeup. You don't know if you like or don't like something until you try it. Two days won't hurt. Be creative so you can find your own identity. Remember, you are a woman, so it's okay to play dress up and let your inner girl out. Men love to see a woman at her best. Find out what styles or colors are your best and try them out!

Cleaning House – Continue to change the house to your liking. Change the furniture around, buy a new chair, bedspread, hang a new picture. Pack up another box of the old to donate. Wash your car, put a new scent in it. Take more pride in yourself, house, and car. Appreciate the blessings you currently have and God will bless you with more.

Treat Yourself – Take an opportunity to go to the movies, see a Broadway show, or attend a concert. Perhaps even buy that new purse you've been eyeing for months, or maybe those expensive shoes you thought were out of your budget.

Spiritual Development and Healing – Walk around your house and pray in each room. Go to your closet and continue to pray for strength. Take a bath, soak, and reflect on your improvements. Journal your experience, your wrongs, your rights, and how your heart truly feels. Spend some time reading a book, something fantastic. Use sticky notes to write down different affirmations or self-proclamations, and make a list of positive adjectives regarding yourself. On those hard days when you cannot think of anything good, or when you see yourself as worthless, choose an affirmation and three of the adjectives and recite them to yourself.

"I will have a great day, no one will interfere with my progress, and I will not allow my spirits to dwell in the negative."

"I am beautiful, intelligent, and funny!"

Congratulations on trying something new and finding yourself. You are on your way.

Phase Four – Forgiveness

Continue on the Journey of Finding Yourself – As stated before, spend two days of the week dressing up, even if you don't have any plans. Wear full makeup and play with colors. Add your favorite scent to your house, like candles, oil diffusers, or even flowers and if you don't have one, find one. Walk outside, detox your body, and fast for a healing spirit.

Spiritual Healing – Ask God to put forgiveness in your heart toward your husband. Write a letter to your husband stating that you are very upset; however, in order to move on, you must forgive him. Be woman enough to apologize in the areas where you lacked as a wife. Forgive yourself, learn from your mistakes, and know and own your truth. Talk to someone of higher authority at your church, such as your pastor or your first lady. Try seeking a therapist or a counselor in confidence to resolve any personal convictions.

Re-Evaluate Your List of Projects – Start a big project on your house, such as painting a room, starting a garden, or buying new furniture. Grab hold of your dreams and begin a new business. Create the plan, seek coaching, and apply for financing. What about building that bookshelf, or adding that extension to your closet or shelving unit for those shoes and purses?

Continue to Treat Yourself – Try something new, such as a full body massage, a Brazilian wax, or a body scrub. Take an adventure and go skiing, skydiving, or polar bearing. If you're feeling daring, take a pilot class, or maybe just take a flight or a cruise.

Guess what? You are creating your new life and learning the new you after hardship.

Girl, get your lyfe…and remember, God loves you.

"Don't stop meeting together with other believers, which some people have gotten into the habit of doing. Instead, encourage each other, especially as you see the day drawing near." Hebrews 10:25 (CEB)

Learning Myself Worksheet

What Makes Me Happy?	Personal Goals
1.	1.
2.	2.
3.	3.
What's My Personality Trait?	Career Goals
1.	1.
What's My Love Language?	2.
1.	3.
What Is Important in a Companion?	What Will I *Not* Accept in a Companion?
1.	1.
2.	2.
3.	3.
Do I Want to Be a Wife?	Am I a Happy Wife?
1.	1.
Do I Want to Be a Mother?	Am I a Happy Mother?
1.	1.

Do I Need a Counselor/Therapist? (Are you able to utilize coping mechanisms to get through stressful days, panic/anxiety attacks, or depression?)	Do I Have Unresolved Issues? (Are you faking it through life?)
1.	1.
5 Positive Attributes of Myself: I am…	**My Favorite Bible Scriptures**
1.	1.
2.	2.
3.	3.
4.	4.
5.	5.

References/Sources Used

Chapman, Gary D. 1995. *The Five Love Languages: How to Express Heartfelt Commitment to your Mate*. Chicago: Northfield Pub.

Common English Bible. CEB Copyright 2010, 2011 by Common English Bible

AM Collins

Bio

A.M. Collins has been reading romance novels since her mother first handed her a Yolanda Joe book. Since then characters' lives have been swirling around in her mind, just waiting to come alive. With life experiences under her belt, A.M. Collins is ready for the world to live with these characters too.

www.ingramcontent.com/pod-product-compliance
Ingram Content Group UK Ltd.
Pitfield, Milton Keynes, MK11 3LW, UK
UKHW022240230426
12048UKWH00018BA/1376